FIX YOUR B.S.
(BELIEF SYSTEMS)

DR. GREG PURSLEY

PUBLISHING

© 2023

Author: Dr. Greg Pursley
Published by: The Ghost Publishing, LLC
Edited by: Eli Gonzalez
Front cover design by Will Figueroa.

Paperback ISBN-13: 979-8-9863992-8-7
Ebook ISBN-13: 979-8-9863992-9-4

CONTENTS

DEDICATION

This book is dedicated to you, the reader. May your life become everything you ever hoped it could be.

GET THE FIX YOUR B.S. BONUS BUNDLE

You can visit

www.FixYourBS.Com/bundle

to get access to Dr. Greg Pursley aka Dr G's bonus bundle which includes:

- The Fix Your B.S. secret bonus chapter "The Biggest Lie Ever Told"
- Exclusive Content with Dr. G
- How to join the Fix Your B.S. community and benefit from Dr G's podcast, social media, and more!

Dr. Greg Pursley aka "Dr G"

FOREWORD BY PETE VARGAS

My world collided with Dr. G's (Greg Pursley) in 2019. I was speaking at Grant Cardone's 10X Growth Con in Miami. I'll never forget that moment when I got introduced and stepped out onto the biggest stage I had ever spoken on in my life. We had packed Marlin's stadium with more than 30,000 ambitious, enthusiastic, and hard-working entrepreneurs. At that moment, I knew I was exactly where I wanted to be. I never knew how I'd get there, I just knew I could and would.

I had never aspired to be a speaker or to coach speakers. That is, until my father heard someone speak from a stage and the words affected him so profoundly that it literally changed his life. Prior to that, my dad and I didn't have a good relationship – at all. It's a terrible thing not to trust or even like the man that is supposed to raise you and teach you what life is all about. The pain and frustration I felt as a teenager were deep and troubling.

But after hearing just one person speak, it changed his life, which changed mine and the trajectory of my family. Now, because of the many stages I've spoken at, and the many amazing individuals I've had the honor to coach, maximizing their talents on stages, such as Tony Robbins, Grant Cardone, Dean Graziosi, Damon John, Ed Mylett, and Brandon Dawson, that person that spoke change into my father's mindset has affected millions and millions of lives for the better.

I thought, I want to do that. I want to help people the way that man helped my father. Then I thought, *who do I think I am? How many people will want to listen to me, a Mexican-born nothing that came from nowhere?*

When my dreams butted heads with my reality, I realized that the battle to be who I wanted to be was with no one else but me. The war for my future was waged in my mind. I promised myself that I would speak on the biggest stages in the world and serve many people and that nothing or no one would stop me.

So there I was, giving my signature talk, not knowing anything about Dr. G. when I offered the attendees an opportunity to take my online course- *Stage to Scale*. That day, unbeknownst to me, Dr. G. became one of my students. However, he soon showed that he wasn't an average student. He was one of a small percentage of people who took that course and played all out. Not only did he take and consume that online course, he then took my Stages Course – twice! He followed that up by becoming a part of my speaking agency – 10X Stages (formerly known as Advance Your Reach).

Having now spent a considerable amount of time with Dr. G., I've seen him improve his craft over time. Through hard work and determination, his ability to elicit emotion and passion from the stage has increased immensely in just four short years. However, just because someone is a great student doesn't guarantee I will write the foreword of their book. I take great care in the people and thoughts I align myself with. After finding out more about him and the contents of this book, I am honored to encourage you to read it. Here's why:

1. There is congruency between what he says and what he does. Dr. G plays all out. He knows what he wants and consistently puts forth the effort, finances, time, and energy to get it. I love people like that!
2. He made a bold claim to me several years ago. He said, "Pete, I'm going to be your most successful student!" Years later, after seeing his growth and commitment, I'm starting to believe that he just might!

As a speaker, my world is full of... talk. People talk a big game. They're not shy to say the great things they're going to do. They brag about what they're going to have. They boast of their dreams, talents, wealth, and future. Some are obnoxious about it and others do it the *humble brag* way. But as the saying goes, *Talk is Cheap*. The results come with the action. Dr. G. has proven to be a massive action-taker. He doesn't just dream it, write it down, and proclaim it – he then plays full out to manifest it.

This book, *Fix your B.S.*, has ideologies that, should you be open to them, have the power to change your life. Dr. G. is a student of some of the brightest minds on the planet, either directly or indirectly (by reading their books, taking their courses, or paying for their one-on-one coaching). He has amassed tried and proven knowledge that has changed many lives, and he then combined it with his own, very unique experiences.

This book will introduce you to five simple steps you can take to get on the path of living the life you dream of. I don't want to tell you what they are yet, you have to read this book to get the full context of it. I will, however, give you a sneak peek without spoiling it – change requires vision, faith, and consistent action.

Sure, change takes work, but then again, what's the alternative? Staying where you are? Miserable? Wanting more out of life but never maximizing your potential?

Dr. G. has the solution. Fix your B.S. and you'll fix your life.

Pete Vargas

1

THE TRUTH WILL SET
YOU FREE

Only the truth of who you are, if realized, will set you free!

— *ECKHART TOLLE*

THE VALUE OF TIME

There are many truths in life—unavoidable, undeniable truths. Then there are truths we thought were absolute, but upon further review, as science and technology and experiences advanced, what we thought were truths became mist in the light of new evidence. Some of them, even after being proven to be false, have formed into superstitions, mindless repetitive behaviors, unfounded "knowledge" passed down from generation to generation.

An absolute truth that will never change, at least in our lifetimes, is that if you were born, you will die, and, right now, you don't know when that's going to be. With that being evidently clear, as you begin to read this book, I want to impress upon you the value of the time you have left, however long that may be.

I heard a quote that has always stuck with me. I probably won't say it word for word, but the meaning is what counts:

If I offered you five million dollars tomorrow morning, would you take it? Sure, you would! However, if I told you that by taking that money, it would be the last day of your life, would you still take it? Of course, not! If you put yourself in that simple analogy, you will have just realized that your time is worth more than $5 million.

If you were to ask any billionaire on his deathbed what he wished he had, he'd say, "More time," as would a millionaire, as would a doctor, as would a janitor, as would a clerk, as would a white person, as would a black person, as would a brown person, as would a heavy-set person, as would a skinny person, as would a male, as would a female, as would…well, you.

Since it is you who is reading this right now, I'd like to come into an agreement with no one other than you. I want us to agree that we are going to take advantage of our time together. I spent years, tears, and a substantial monetary investment during the course of my life to discover the life-changing revelations I share in this book. What you are holding is evidence of how I've spent my valuable time. My intention is to help you compress time by learning from my life and experiences so that you may be able to utilize and maximize your present time so that your future time can be lived how you desire.

What I want you to agree to is to capitalize on your time reading this by doing two things. First, grab a highlighter and highlight the parts of the book that jump into your soul. Analyze them. Digest them. Memorize them. Quote them. Secondly, and more importantly, I'd like you to commit to taking consistent action on the parts of this book that touch you. Consistency is more important than intensity. I'd rather work out three times a week at 60 percent intensity every week without fail than work out at 110 percent intensity, randomly and inconsistently. Consistency breeds habits; new, positive habits breed positive change; positive change breeds rewards; rewards breed more motivation; more motivation breeds consistency.

Another absolute truth is that during the time between being born and dying, we're all going to have struggles. Know this: life is struggle. You will experience pain, sorrow, remorse, heartbreak, and turmoil. While it's never pleasant, it's necessary. You cannot grow without it. So, you have two choices on how to deal with those situations: react to it and be at its whim, or expect it and handle it. It is going to happen! So, knowing that it's going to happen, when it does, simply ask yourself, "What can I learn from this?" The more times you struggle and learn, the fewer struggles you will have next time. This is called: experience.

If you've picked up this book, chances are it's because there is something inside of you that keeps nagging and gnawing at you, telling you: *I should be better by now. I should have more (friends, houses, material possessions, etc.). I should have done more with my life by now. I should have more money than I have. I should have started my business already. My business should have exploded by now. I should have lost that weight by now. I should know what my reason for being is by now. I should have* (fill in your personal frustration here) _____.

CAN YOU HANDLE THE TRUTH?

I'm going to tell you why you are frustrated, but you have to be prepared to face the ugly truth. You are frustrated because

3

you know you are capable of doing more, being more, and experiencing more, but you have been afraid of taking action.

So, you make up reasons (excuses) in your mind that hold you back.

To prepare you to brace for this bitter truth, it's best if you learn the Double V technique.

When there's a disagreement between two people, the Double V technique requires one of them to say his/her *truth or their reality as he/she sees it.* The other person has to write down what he's hearing. He is not allowed to stop the person talking, he can't explain anything, he can't throw the pen and pad at the person talking; he can only write down what he's getting. Once the other person is done, the person who wrote tells the person who spoke what he got from it. If the person who spoke wasn't completely understood, he continues to talk and the other person continues to write until the person who was speaking is satisfied and feels he/she was heard.

Then, and only then, do they switch roles, and the person who talked now writes while the person who wrote gets to talk, uninterrupted. They do this until the person now writing can express what the person now talking is saying. Clear communication has a way of establishing peace or, at least, if there is still a disagreement, turning it into a newfound respect for the other person's perspective.

Every argument comes from miscommunication and/or unmet expectations. Communication is an exchange of ideas and information. If your viewpoint and expectations are never communicated concisely, disagreements will occur. If you are too afraid to communicate to be understood, the situation and emotions will get out of control and will eventually put you in situations you'd rather not be in.

In the same way, I'd like for you to hold back your pride, your reasons (excuses), and the internal mental rebuttals that are going to want to protect your ego. Just read to understand; don't read to waste time or make sense of your situation. If you don't like your current situation, you will need to have different information and habits in order to create a new situation. Deal?

Cool.

Now, here is the ugly truth. The reason you are frustrated in your current life is nobody's fault but your own. It's not the divorce; it's not the bad partner; it's not the lawsuit; it's not the government; it's not your pastors; it's not your mother, father, brother, sister, wife, husband, boyfriend, girlfriend; or the era in which you were born. It's not the pandemic, politics, or anything outside of what is between your ears. The reason you have not done what you feel you should have done by now is because of your belief systems, your conclusions, your script, and fear.

DEBILITATING SCRIPTS AND BELIEF SYSTEMS

Your scripts and belief systems are the documented account of your life as you perceive it. Allow me to explain how this works. Let's say you went on a date, and, without conscious thought, you scripted what you liked about the other person and what you didn't, and that determined if you went on a second date. You have a script based on every experience that has formed you into being the person you are today.

You are who you are today based on who your script says you are. You may have made decisions when you were ten years old and are now using that decision as a filter to make decisions today. At that time, you couldn't even make decisions for yourself, such as what you'd wear, what you'd eat, or where you'd go. Your parents made those decisions for you. Yet, you formulated an inner script that has been the foundation or baseline for your decisions today. Decisions made by ten-year-olds don't work out well for twenty-, thirty-, forty-, or fifty-year-olds.

It is time to look inwardly and analyze and question your current beliefs; otherwise, you won't grow. Ask yourself:

- *What do I believe about money, relationships, faith, health, and a career?*
- *What am I capable of?*
- *What if I had zero limitations?*

I want you to imagine the life you would like to live. Make it as clear as you can in your mind's eye. Allow yourself to hear the sounds you want to hear, whether it's the sound of the waves, being at an opera, little children playing in the background. What does your home look like? How is it decorated? Go outside or down to the adjacent garage and look at the car you own. Dream without limits. Let your imagination crystalize into something nearly tangible, tasteful, and audible. Be honest with yourself. If it's the ego that has to paint the picture, let it paint while your humility and limitations' look at your version of a living masterpiece materialize. BE HONEST—I can't express this strongly enough. Dream. Soar. It might be the first time you ever truthfully answered this question: what do you want out of life? In order to manifest the picture in your mind, it may be time to rewrite your script.

Your script, like scripture that you write or religious Scripture you believe, is as true to you as the air you breathe. Your script tells you if you're good at this or good at that. It tells you if you'll quit when the going gets tough. It predetermines the exact moment you give up on something, someone, or yourself. If you aren't happy with yourself, it's time to flip the script!

The bad news is this: Changing your script, who your subconscious says you are, is not easy. It took consistent action that turned into the habits that made you become who you are. The good news is this: You created your current script, and you have the power to recreate a better one. You are fully in control of you, which is evidenced by the life you currently have. You may not consciously know it, but you are currently living the life you think you deserve. You might want to argue with my last line (read it again), but give me a moment to explain...read me out.

The world in front of you is the world you've focused on. If you've focused on hoping you don't get divorced, you're probably divorced or in a bad marriage. It's like if you're carrying a glass of water filled to the brim. If you think, "Don't spill, water; don't spill," chances are you're more inclined to spill it than if you said, "Stay in the cup, water; stay in the cup."

If you focus on the negative issues in this world, you'll experience them more often. If you focus on scarcity, you'll find yourself lacking. If you focus on someone taking your position, you'll inevitably sit on the bench. However, if you focus on the belief that things don't happen *to* you, they happen *for* you, you'll see opportunities where others see negativity. If you focus on abundance, you'll find yourself in a position to bless others. If you focus on doing your job to the best of your abilities, you'll be irreplaceable.

I don't know if this all seems easy or difficult; either way, you'd be right. If you think it's easy, it'll be easier than if you think it would be difficult. The battle, my friend, is deeper than just in your mind; people change their minds all the time. Your script, the record of your accumulative experiences, is deep in your subconscious, right down to your soul. But, if you believe as I do, there is hope. Souls get saved!

I love this quote from Steve Harvey: "God don't deliver on any other street than Faith Street. He don't deliver on It Might

Happen Street, I Don't Think I Can Do That Street, or Maybe Next Time Street. He delivers on Faith Street."

I'm asking you to have faith that you will become the person you have always wanted to be. This doesn't matter if your faith is in God, the universe, yourself, or if you have faith in none of it. You have to at least have faith in yourself. Faith and Hope are powerful friends in the journey to self-realization and dream-life-manifestation. Just know this: Having faith or hope won't change your life by themselves. Creating a vision board or speaking declarations every morning won't change your life by themselves. It takes action—consistent action. It's consistently doing the small things in a big way all the time.

A LITTLE ABOUT DR. G.

In the following chapter, I'm going to introduce to you the five-step process that has taken me a lifetime to discover. Focusing on these five areas has helped me tremendously. I had been a business owner for thirteen years, and I was frustrated and in debt. I'm a doctor! That's not supposed to happen to people like me. Yet, there I was, Dr. Greg Pursley—worried sick on how I was going to continue to provide for my family and how to enjoy my life more. I hated being stuck in the day-to-day grind of trying to figure out what I wanted, let alone how to get it.

I realized I needed help from people who had done what I wanted to do.

I made the decision to go to a business conference—except there was a problem. I didn't have the money or the available credit.

The more I thought about the conference, the more I wanted to go, and therefore, the more I focused on going. Two weeks after making the decision that I was going to this conference no matter what, Discover Card sent me a $20,000 no-interest line of credit. I took action on my decision to go to the conference, and, somehow, convinced my wife that I should use that money to go. (It's great to have an understanding partner who has faith in you; even when they don't understand, they see your passion and agree.)

I went to the conference, committed to take action on the opportunities and relationships that would become available. I met some great people, one of whom helped me with this very book! I invested in four programs: John Maxwell's Leadership Program, Jesse Itzler's Build Your Life Resumé Program, Pete Vargas's Stage to Scale Program, and Grant Cardone's Cardone U. I returned home with most of the $20,000 converted into more debt. However, I felt I finally had the resources to change my life.

It didn't happen overnight. Nothing that lasts usually does. I woke up early every morning and did the work. Nothing changed. I made a conscious decision to keep doing it and build new habits. Over time, it seeped into the fabric of who I am. Still, though, I had not experienced a magical transformation. Then, about a year after, my wife commented on how she saw a huge growth and change in me. It was then that I realized the secret: just keep going!

My income, my happiness, and my zeal for life all increased. I felt I was finally headed somewhere. I wasn't there yet—still not close, actually—but I was moving in the right direction. I made the decision to go to the same event the following year, except that this time, I had money. I invested even more to get me closer to the speakers, people I had selected to mentor me. Had I been inconsistent in taking the courses, I would not have had the communication skills required for them to notice me and take me seriously. Again, I invested more time and money with them. The following year, my income quadrupled.

As I reflected on my journey, who I was before and who I was now becoming, I identified the five areas of my life I had focused on that changed my life. It was then that I felt compelled to write this book. If it worked for me, it can work for you, so long as you, too, are committed to taking consistent action.

Contained in this book are answers you've been searching for. Many of them have been hidden in plain sight. I haven't invented any words for this book; it's not that complicated. But I will guarantee you this: should you take consistent action on what I teach herein, it will change your life. God won't do it. The Universe won't do it. Your connections won't do it. Changing your life is all up to you. Turn the page and find out how.

ACTION STEPS:

What are some of the beliefs that hold you back?

What actions do you know you should take that you have taken to improve your life?

2

DR. G'S FIVE PILLARS OF LIFE

Those who have a "why" to live can bear with almost any "how."

— *VIKTOR FRANKLE*

GET COMFORTABLE BEING UNCOMFORTABLE

Growing as a person happens in two different ways. In terms of physically growing from an infant to an adult, it's a natural process. You don't have to do anything but tend to your core needs: eat, drink water, and sleep. You don't need to bathe, work out, or be kind to anyone; just eat and sleep, and your body will change over time.

It is vastly more challenging to grow into a person who reaches his or her potential. That requires intentional and consistent action. The reality is this: nothing will change in your life until you take action. The main reason people don't take action to become what they wish they could become, or have the ability to become, or even to find out what their limits are, is because they aren't willing to get uncomfortable. They would rather stay where they are, complain about it, and then not do anything about it except complain about it again.

Human beings carry incredible wonder and power within them, yet most would rather remain where they are—ordinary and unfulfilled, and I call it "settling." People have so much potential, but they let it go to waste. It baffles me. Settling is one of the greatest travesties people do to themselves!

There are people who would love to get in shape and have more defined muscles, but they don't work out because they get sore or they repeat to themselves, "I'll just quit like last time." They don't lose weight because they don't want to feel hungry. They don't have great relationships because they're unwilling to have the tough conversations that need to be had.

Too many people allow themselves to get scared away from living their dream lives by something that MIGHT happen

So, they remain where they are, uncomfortable that they have many issues and wishing they could have a better life, yet unwilling to be uncomfortable on the journey to getting it.

So, you see, you can either be uncomfortable while building a life that you'd eventually be proud of and comfortable in, or stay uncomfortable while complaining about the life you have and never fixing it. It is up to you to decide if there are things in your life you wish were different. If there are, it's your choice if you're willing to get uncomfortable to remedy the situation.

Serial entrepreneur and multi-millionaire Brandon Dawson talks about the Three Ts to growth. The first T is Transactional. This is when conversations are very surface-level, like buying a pack of gum at a gas station:

"How you doin'?"

"Good."

"That'll be two dollars and twenty-five cents. Cash or card?"

"Card."

Relationships can't grow through transactional conversations. There's no depth in "How's the weather going to be tomorrow" conversations.

The second T is Transition. This is the journey I challenge you to embark on as you read this book. This is when you realize that, maybe, you've been blaming other people or organizations or the government for your woes. This is when you get so sick and tired of going through the same B.S., and you get upset with yourself because you have yet to even scratch the surface of your potential, that you decide to change and take action. The difficulty with this step is that it makes people uncomfortable.

The third T is Transformation. To transform into the person you want to be, first, you need to figure out who that is. It is foolish to continue to do everything you do now and expect to become who you want to be. Doing what you've done is what made you who you are now. Doing more of the same won't change anything. Something has to change. Something has to go away. If you want to be a millionaire, you have to stop hanging out with people who just want to get by. In order to transform, you need to change your beliefs: what you believe you are capable of, a higher power, the manifestation of destiny, and what you see in your mind's eye.

There's a saying: Leaders are Readers. Why? Because they continue to receive new information, and, based on those new ideas, they take new action. The new action provides them with new, better results. Other people see how they've changed and then decide to follow them. Some of the best leaders don't intentionally want to lead; they just aren't willing to settle for a life less than what they're capable of living, and people resonate with strong-willed people who don't settle for less. So, they read to find out the answers to the things they don't yet know.

Being uncomfortable is akin to paying the toll to get on the road that can get to where you want to go faster. When you first rode a bike, you were uncomfortable and probably scared as hell. But you didn't stop, even though you may have wrecked a few times. You may not have ridden a bike for thirty years, but if you get on one, you'll be able to ride it. Why? Because you have gone past the uncomfortable emotions of riding a bike, and now, that which made you uncomfortable is comfortable.

You have to understand that being uncomfortable when doing something new eventually turns into a common thing. I had always loved books and admired authors, but I was never an avid reader. Once I realized that my mission in life is to find out what I'm capable of, I created a habit of reading or listening to books. It has become an identifier. If you come to my practice and find me missing, this is probably what you'd hear:

"Where's Dr. G?"

"Probably listening to a book somewhere."

Books have become a necessary part of my life. My employees would sometimes ask me, "What book did you get this week?"

I am on the journey of becoming who I know I can be now because of the books I've consumed. However, books were never part of my everyday routine. I've realized that I don't have all the answers and sometimes don't even have the best questions—so, I search for them. I glean insight into things from experts that shorten the learning curve for me. They inspire me and excite me to the point where I'm compelled to take action. In short, you don't know what you don't know.

BEWARE OF "BECAUSE"

A woman told me that she wanted to go on a cruise. She has the time and the money to go on whichever cruise she chooses. I told her, "Book it; you have the time and the money." She said she couldn't because she had nobody to go with. It's been several years since that simple conversation, and she still wishes she would go on a cruise but has never been on one. She justified and concluded why she couldn't go "because" she didn't have anyone to go with. This is how your brain works. She told herself she had no one to go with, and her brain said, "Okay, you can't go on a cruise." She probably never considered to find someone to go with. Her *because* became her reality.

Has anyone ever mentioned to you something they wished they would have done or would do and then told you the reason why they didn't or won't do it? There's an expression that goes like this: Anything after the word "because" is bullshit. Have you heard it? Sadly, that expression is too true to too many people. The word "because" is often a precursor to an excuse that people call a "reason." When someone tells you they can't lose weight, you ask why, and they say, "Because my knees hurt and I can't run." Is that a reason, or an excuse? I would follow up the person's statement with this question: "Are there other ways to lose weight?" I'll expect you to ask yourself similar questions later in this book.

On your quest to live out loud, the comfort zone you're in will implant a lot of *reasons* you shouldn't even get started on the journey. Challenge your "reasons." They are what have held you down for so long!

I believe the only way to have a shot at living your dream life is first to understand what type of life that is, and then challenge your excuses and take consistent action.

Now, let's get to my five pillars of life. I believe a full, happy life is based on five major areas. Here they are, in no particular order:

1. Relationships
2. Career
3. Finances
4. Health
5. Faith

As you delve deeper into this journey with me, you'll be able to identify how important each of those five pillars is in a way that will move you to action. If you can find joy in fulfillment in each of those areas, you're rocking it as a human being in this century. If any of these are off, you are not living the best life possible. If all of them are bad, well, we've got a lot of work to do.

ACTION STEPS:

Write down all the "Reasons" why you have said you can't get what you want?

Write down the TRUTH.

Write down the different statements that will get you want you want:

3

THE FIVE STEPS TO
IMPROVING YOUR LIFE

You can't drift your way to the top of the mountain.

— *JIM ROHN*

ARE YOU READY?

This is the part of the book where it becomes interactive if you are serious about living up to your potential. I'm going to give you five easy-to-do and reasonable exercises that literally have the power to change your life and shift you to the path of whatever success and happiness mean to you.

These steps require the following:

1. For you to be honest and transparent with yourself, who you are, and who you want to be
2. A pen and paper
3. Consistent action

If you do these three things, I promise you will see results, as will those closest to you.

STEP 1: VISION

Take a glimpse into the future and write down your ideal situation in the five central pillars of life: relationships, career, finances, health, and faith. Define what each would look like. In a perfect world, how would your relationships be with your spouse, children, boss, employees, friends, colleagues, etc.? Write it out—but here's the hidden power: write it down in the present tense, as if you are currently enjoying those relationships in real time. For example:

WRONG: My wife and I will be going on walks every morning.
RIGHT: My wife and I enjoy our morning walks.

WRONG: I will run my own business and have three
employees.
RIGHT: I walk into my shop and bring my three employees
coffee every morning.

WRONG: I will have $3,000 in the bank, and I'll also own a
vacation property that makes me money every month.
RIGHT: I have $3,000 in the bank, and I make a $2,000 profit
every month with my vacation property on Clearwater Beach,
Florida.

WRONG: I will go to the gym three times a week and go for
runs twice a week. I'll also eat healthier and only drink alcohol
on the weekends.
RIGHT: I work out at the gym three times a week, and I run
two miles twice a week when I don't go to the gym. I don't
consume nearly as much sugar, and I only drink alcohol on
weekends, and that's only if I'm at a social function.

WRONG: I will believe in myself more than ever before. I will not be scared to take risks.
RIGHT: I believe in myself more than ever before, and I'm no longer afraid to take risks.

Write down how you would like every relationship that matters to you as if it were your current reality. Write down the career you want to have as if you already have it. Write down how you want your finances to be as if they are. Write down the healthy lifestyle you want to live as if you're living it. Write down the faith you have in yourself or a higher power as if you possess it right now.

Don't mind the gap between the present you and the future you. If your focus is on the distance to get there, you'll never make it.

*Just focus on what you want,
not on how you'll get it.*

The first battle is won in your head; winning the war comes after.

STEP 2: WHY

Come to terms with why you want it. You don't have to be Mr. or Mrs. Noble. If your "why" is to prove others wrong, own it! Being congruent with your authentic "why" is what will give you the emotional fuel that will drive you through the tougher parts of your journey. Challenge yourself. For example, if you want to lose twenty pounds, ask yourself why.

To feel better.

Good. What does it matter for you to feel better?

I'll be able to spend more time outside with my young children.

Nice. How would that impact your children's lives?

They'll see me prioritize them by spending quality time with them doing what they like to do.

Very nice. Why is that important?

They'll know how important they are to me and have a stronger sense of self-worth.

Tell me, which would help you go through the hunger pains and make you exercise more—wanting to feel better, or so that your kids know they're important to you so that they have a stronger sense of self-worth?

The transformational journey you are about to embark on requires grit and consistency. Understanding the inner workings of your unique self and owning your "why" is vital to becoming the person you want to be.

STEP 3: WRITE DOWN THE HABITS THAT DRIVE YOU TOWARD YOUR VISION

If you have a weight loss goal, what are you doing right now that helps you lose weight? Are you drinking a lot of water? Great. Write that down. Do you go for walks? Great. Write that down.

The gap will seem smaller once you realize that you're not starting at ground zero. You're already doing things to get you to your ideal life. Did you start doing date nights with your spouse once a month? Great. Write it down. Do you make your kids breakfast on Sunday mornings? Do you save 10 percent of your earnings on an account you don't touch? Have you gone to a business conference to learn from masters in business? It's easier to *keep* doing something or to do a little more of something than to *start* doing something.

STEP 4: 4. WRITE NEW HABITS THAT WILL MOVE YOU TOWARD YOUR GOAL/VISION AND TAKE IMMEDIATE ACTION

If you have a weight loss goal, but constantly snack on chips and ice cream, write it down. Do you drink alcohol four times a week and, as a result on many workdays, it takes you till 10 a.m. to feel like your normal self and function properly? Write it down.

Be honest with yourself. It's time for you to stop believing the B.S. excuses you've come to accept as valid reasons. Challenge whatever comes after the word "because."

People complain that they don't have money for important things, yet they find the money for their hobbies. I know a guy who couldn't pay the rent but bought an expensive crossbow. When his landlord asked him how he could afford the crossbow and not the rent, the man said his mother helped him pay for it. The landlord asked, "Maybe your mother would have preferred to help you pay for the roof over your head so you don't live on the street?"

The truth is this: all of the necessary resources you need to live the life you want are at your disposal. Some things will take you time to grow into, but things you can do now will get you there. However, if you believe your B.S. excuses, you'll stay where you are, complaining about your life for the rest of your life. So for this step, write down everything that holds you back; don't give yourself a pass. Don't blame the divorce, inflation, government, etc. Identify your bad habits and put them on paper. By knowing what they are, the enemy to your best life is no longer hidden and can now be fought.

STEP 5: CIRCLE ONE THING THAT'S CURRENTLY MOVING YOU AWAY FROM YOUR GOAL AND CHOOSE A DIFFERENT HABIT.

I'm not asking you to change your life dramatically all at once. You eat an elephant one bite at a time, not in one gulp. Take something you've identified in step 4. Let's say you drink alcohol five times a week, then you get hungry and eat late at night. Choose another habit instead. Choose to only drink one day a week with friends and only have a couple of drinks. If you started to implement this new habit, which you could, if you were connected with your "why," you might come to some life-changing crossroads: *Why am I going out again? I'm spending money, laughing at the same jokes with the same people at the same places.* Soon after, you might tally up your monthly bar tab and realize what you could have bought instead and quit drinking alcohol altogether.

If you can identify and double-down on the good habits that drive you to your goal and replace a bad habit with another good practice that also drives you toward your goals, you'll quickly pick up momentum. You'll feel as if a great weight has fallen off your shoulders and you will find certainty instead of confusion. Brandon Dawson says, "A confused mind will always lead to failure." The clearer you are, the more success you will have.

After reading this chapter, don't ever allow yourself to believe the excuse that you don't know how to change your life. The steps are right here. They work, but only if you work them.

ACTION STEPS:

1. What are you justifying with "because"?
2. What is your vision in all five pillars of life?

3. What habits take you toward and away from your
   vision?

4
THE PURSUIT OF HAPPINESS

---

*"Everyone chases after happiness, not noticing that happiness
is right at their heels."*

— BERTOLT BRECHT – PLAYWRIGHT
AND POET

THE TRUTH ABOUT THE PURSUIT OF HAPPINESS

Recently, I saw a dog chasing its tail. It's not the first time I've
seen it; most likely, you've seen that as well. It's a comical sight.
The dog goes around in circles like a cyclone, nipping and bark-
ing, without ever catching its tail. I mention it because this latest
time, I wanted to communicate with the dog and tell it, "If you
just stand still and stop going in circles, you can catch your tail!"
Unfortunately, dog-whispering is not a part of my skill set, so I
walked on, and the dog kept spinning like a top.

In the same manner, humans chase after happiness. Only, it's not
as comical of a sight; it's a sad one.

I'll be happy when I get married.
I'll be happy when I lose thirty pounds.
I'll be happy when I'm a millionaire.
I'll be happy when I graduate, when I get that job, when I get that
house, when I get that car, when I go on vacation to Rome,
when I...

They take the happiness that, as Bertolt quoted, is at their heels, and place it in an unreachable place: the future. That's just not a smart way to live a happy life. The problem then compounds because they make it a habit of doing that, so when they get married or lose the weight or graduate—they set another goal and never fully experience the happiness they sought for so long. It slips from their grasp and their current reality, once more, is devoid of a happy, enjoyable life.

You have to understand that you won't find true or lasting happiness when you reach a goal. Sure, you might get excited, do a few fist-pumps, go out and celebrate, or go to sleep with a huge, smug grin on your face. But then, sooner or later, the new car loses its new-car smell, the promise of being a doctor turns into eighty-hour work weeks, or the extra money birthed in you a taste for finer things and you still don't have extra money like you wanted to, even though you're making more than ever.

Some people don't bother having goals. They had some before, but never reached them, so they'll distract themselves with alcohol to not face the depression they're in. They fool themselves into believing that having big goals would just make them depressed. Life happens *to* them and not *for* them, providing excuse after excuse to convert into reason after reason why they're good right where they are. Sound familiar? It's okay; I've been there too.

Whether you're a goal setter or not, know this: happiness isn't found in reaching the goal. Happiness is found in the doing.

Happiness is found in progress. Happiness is found in knowing that you are closer to your goal today than you were yesterday. When you find it there, your life will improve dramatically.

I read a great book called *The One Thing* by Gary W. Keller and Jay Papasan, which I highly recommend. In it, he wrote, "What's the one thing I can do, such that by doing it, everything else will be easier or unnecessary?" When you can develop the habit of being present and taking action that brings you closer to who you want to be or what you want to have, you'll live a happier life. Don't you think that's worth it?

The One Thing also got me to understand that we all have the same amount of time, but if we learn to continuously become more impactful (create good habits) with the time we have, and learn to be present and excited in being in the moment, life gets better—in your present as well as your future.

I'm a believer in delayed gratification, but not with everything. If you were saving up for a specific car, I would advise you to not buy the first car you see just because you can afford it. I'd recommend you save up for a few more months and get the car you really want. That, to me, is delayed gratification.

But to delay on happiness
doesn't make sense to me,
at all.

Happiness shouldn't *be* a long-term goal; it should ride *with you* in the car toward the goal.

Personally, I've set goals that may be widely ridiculous compared to the average individual. I have not reached many of them yet, but I wake up with great enthusiasm every day now because each day I do at least one thing that gets me closer to my big, hairy, audacious goals.

You'll read a few recurring themes in this book, probably none more than: you have to take action. If you aren't willing to take action, this book, and any like it, are pointless. Before you take action, though, you need to know what actions to take and why. In order to do that, you need to know your goals.

What are your goals? Write them down. Challenge yourself to write out the true desires of your heart. Your heart doesn't think small; your fear does. Gary Keller says, *"Don't let small thinking cut your life down to size. Think big, aim high, act bold. And see just how big you can blow up your life."*

Grant Cardone wrote in his book *The 10X Rule*—and I'm paraphrasing here—if your goal is to make $100K a year, you'll have to hit 100 percent of your goal in order to make 100K/year. Set a new goal of making $1 million a year. That would force you to think differently and take new, never-before-done action. You may not reach the $1 million a year, but you may end up at $500K a year, crushing your original $100K goal. So, even though I may not reach all of my big, hairy, audacious goals, or as Pete Vargas calls them, "B'HAGs," I'm still going to be wildly successful and immensely happy, because I will have still maximized my potential, served a lot of people, and made my mark on this earth with the time I've been given.

Remember, the happiness is not in the goal. On your way to achieving your goal, you may find that it morphs into something entirely different. It was your heart's true desire all along, but you had to get a higher vantage point and experience different things to even consider it as an alternative.

Progress equals happiness. Enjoy the progress, and you'll enjoy more moments.

YOUR BRAIN ISN'T YOU

Many people are confused with who they are. Not who they want to become and who others say they are; they don't themselves know who they are. Meaning: they think that they are their brains and their brains are them, that their brains hold the master controls of what they do and how they behave. That, my friends, although it seems right, is simply not true.

The brain is an organ, like the heart and the kidneys. It's the center of the nervous system. Your brain's sole job is to keep you alive. It will try to protect you from harmful, hurtful, and stressful situations. For example: if you go running, at some point during the run, your brain will collect data from your body and conclude that you are tired—not that *it* is tired, but that *your body* is tired. It concludes that if you keep up the activity, eventually, your body will break down, which is what the brain is there to ensure does not happen. In reaction to the body's stress, it will tell you that you've had enough running for the day; stop now, and run again another day.

At that particular juncture, you can either adhere to the brain's recommendation and stop running, or you can tell it that you have some fitness goals to reach and tell it to shut up. That's when the real you reveals itself, your soul. It dominates the brain and forces the body to keep running.

Never blindly trust your brain or the first thought that pops up in your head. Thoughts of fear, worry, and doubt come unbidden to your subconscious. That's when your conscious mind has to challenge whether what your brain is thinking or suggesting you do is valid, or if it's just based on baseless fears or superstitions.

Never forget that you are in control of you and that you can tell your brain to shut up with that nonsense it's trying to get you to act on or not. Be aware of your thoughts and question them. Former Navy Seal, ultra-marathon runner, ultra-distance cyclist, public speaker, and best-selling author David Goggins says:

> *"The feeling that you're completely tapped out actually comes when you're only 40 percent done; you still have 60 percent left in the tank."*

Your brain will try to keep you out of stressful situations, and stress comes in different forms: mental, physical, emotional, and chemical. Many times, or maybe even most times, it will be right. However, it loves the status quo. It loves being comfortable. When you push it to think on higher things and to take new action, it doesn't like it. It will try to reason with you; that's when you allow faith to come into the picture and shut down its argument.

Faith and Brain don't always see eye to eye. Brain needs to see it first; it wants to stay doing what it knows it knows how to do, and it thinks that you can't teach an old dog new tricks. Faith is a different breed because it is based on imagination and projection. Faith will believe in something unseen. Faith will believe in something never before done. Faith will believe that you can live a much bigger, more impactful, and happier life. Which one wins? The one you feed.

If you listen to your brain when it tells you to stay in the comfort zone, and if you're fortunate enough to live to be eighty years old and you find yourself rocking on a rocking chair, you'll have more regrets than you have wrinkles.

I should have done this…
I should have done that…
I should have said this…

I wish I would have…
I bet I could have…

I don't know about you, but I'd rather live with the pain of maximizing my potential over the pain of regret, of knowing that I was too much of a coward to not even try.

Tony Robbins has a great exercise to do to counter when your brain tells you not to do something or that you can't do something. First, ask yourself: *What would I have to believe for that to be true?* For example, let's say your brain tells you that you can't run five miles.

Ask yourself: *What would I have to believe for that to be true?*
Answer: *I would have to ultimately believe that a person of my age and health could never run five miles.*
Ask yourself: *Has anyone my age with my health ever done it?*
Answer: *Yes.*
Ask yourself: *What challenges did they have to overcome?*
Answer: *They had to eat better and start off by walking, then walking and running, then running a mile, then three, and then five miles.*
Ask yourself: *Is it possible for me to do that?*
Answer: *Yes.*
Ask yourself: *Do I believe I'm worth it?*
Answer: *Hell, yeah!*

ACTION STEPS:

Write down something you think you would never be able to do:

Ask yourself: What would I have to believe for that to be true?

Answer:

Ask yourself: Has anyone ever done it?

Answer:

Ask yourself: What challenges did they try to overcome?

Answer:

Ask yourself: Is it possible for me to do that?

Answer:

Ask yourself: Do I deserve it?

Answer:

Be brave. You can create the life you want.

5

SELFISH VS. SELF-LOVE

"Have no fear of perfection—you'll never reach it."

— *SALVADOR DALI*

IMPERFECT VISION

Many people think they know what they want out of life, but for most people, their vision is blurry, at best. They say they want land or they want a sports car or they want to make more money. I've learned, through mentors, through reading, and through my experiences, that the clearer you are when expressing what you want out of life, the better chance you have of obtaining it.

The subconscious mind is incredibly powerful. It will pick up on the information you intentionally give it, and it will allow you to be sensitive to the resources around you to get it. It will put you in front of people who can move you toward your goal. It will remind you of a friend you haven't spoken to in years who has access to the title of a person you need to speak with. Like radar, it will detect people, places, and things that you come into proximity to, but then, it's up to you to pick up on it and capitalize on it. In a way, it works much like when you buy a car: you start noticing other cars like yours.

So, instead of saying you want land, clarify the vision. Where do you want it? Out on the open plains? In a city? Near a lake? Hilly or smooth grass or near a protected forest with many trees? What type of sports car do you want? A Ferrari? An F-Type Jaguar? What year? What color? New or used? If you say you want to make more money...okay, how much more? If you made just one dollar more than last year, you've made more money. Do you want to make $100K? $350K? A million? Be specific with what you want out of your life; create the strategy on how to get it, execute the strategy consistently, and trust that something greater than you will help you get it.

The problem, at times, is that what you think you want is not what you really want. I was coaching a client, and we were going over his goals. As he wrote them out, he listed a Ferrari. I asked him why he wanted it (as I mentioned before, without knowing your "why," you'll be running on fumes before long), and he said that as a kid, he always had Ferrari posters on his wall and that it had been his dream car for as long as he could remember.

"I get it," I said. "Have you ever ridden in one?"

"No."

"Sat in one or touched one?"

"No."

I advised him to go to the Ferrari dealer and take one out for a test drive and listen to the engine, pull the levers, and punch it to see if he liked it and if he could handle the speed. He did exactly that, and it turned out that he found the seats uncomfortable. Shortly after that, he purchased an Aston Martin. He wanted the idea of "Ferrari," but not the Ferrari itself.

I was talking to a bright nineteen-year-old college kid who was a finance major. He told me his goal was to be a CPA, but not very enthusiastically. I asked him why, and he said he wanted to be a CPA because he'd always been good with numbers, and it made sense.

"Have you ever talked to a CPA and asked what he or she likes and doesn't like about being one?"

"No."

Do you see the pattern here? Many people create a belief about a potential reality that's not real in the sense that we only think of the good things, the highlights. People want to be doctors to be rich, buy big boats, golf, and travel, but they don't think of the fact that many doctors work so many hours that a law had to be put in place to prevent doctors from working more than eighty hours a week. They don't think of the emotional component of telling a mother and father that their seven-year-old daughter passed away. They don't realize they would be dealing with people during the worst moments of their lives, as is the case with Emergency Room physicians. They have no idea the emotional rollercoaster attached to those big checks.

As you create the vision for your best future, don't overlook the negative things that come with your goals—no one's life is perfect. If you believe in yourself that you can do something, find someone who is already doing what you think you want to do and get a complete picture before you start painting on life's canvas.

THE OTHERS

If you have a big, hairy, audacious goal, most likely, you're going to need help reaching it. Rome wasn't built in a day, nor did one person build it. Lucky for you, you live in an age where you have all the information you need at your fingertips.

Mentorship is not restricted to hiring a life or business coach. It's also more than just going to conferences, reading books, or taking courses from people you respect. It can also be taking people out to lunch who have what you want to have. Ask them about their favorite topic—them! Take copious notes. If you don't, and if you make it to the goal you think you want, you could very well lose your luster for life instead of relishing it. The less famous the people are, the more accessible they are.

Proximity is powerful. As I began this new journey of manifesting my full potential, I put myself in close proximity with the people I want to be associated with: the biggest speakers; philanthropists; and highly influential, high-net-worth individuals. Before that, however, I read their books, saw their YouTube videos, and sat amongst thousands of people at their conferences. I did what they taught and found more success, so much so that I didn't have to sit in the back row at the conferences; I could finally sit at the front and, as a VIP, walk confidently past the velvet rope to actually get their attention.

When I spoke with them, I didn't do so as a fan. A fan is someone who runs up to someone ("Oh my god!") and throws a book in the celebrity's face, begging for a signature, and nearly passes out when the book is handed back signed. Because I consumed their content, when I met them, I spoke their language. I had the privilege of meeting someone I had followed closely. Although I was excited, and my heart wanted to beat out of my chest and turn me into a raving fan, I knew the moment was too important to waste it gushing when I could be learning and forging. So, after I shook his hand and we exchanged the usual pleasantries, I asked him, "In page 234, you wrote something very interesting that I'd love for you to expand on really quickly. You wrote…"

It was as if he looked at me as a person, and not as a fan, for the first time. I was happy to realize that he was willing to give information and time to people who are intelligently excited, intentional, and ready to learn. There's a saying about not meeting your heroes because they'll not live up to what you thought of them in your head. However, I met some heroes, and they remain heroes—and now, friends. I learned this from John Maxwell.

Tony Robbins says that finding the right mentors, the right people to learn from, turns decades into days. After all, there are two ways to grow:

1. Your experiences
2. Someone else's experiences

Learning from your own experiences is the best way to learn, except that it's a lot more painful and it takes a hell of a lot more time.

A reporter once asked an aging billionaire how he became so successful.

The rich man told him, "By making the right decisions."

The reporter asked how he knew how to make the right decisions.

The rich man told him, "Experience."

The reporter asked him how he got experience.

The rich man answered, "By making many wrong decisions."

Choose your mentors wisely, and then, pay the price by wisely doing what they tell you. Or, pay the price and take the long way around.

COMPARING KILLS DRIVE

A few years ago, I had made a decision to get in much better physical condition. I began working out six days a week. I'd do HITT training three days and weight-lift at the gym three days. That, along with a good diet, gave me results quickly. One day, I was jogging around my neighborhood and saw some neighbors hanging out, having a few beers. They waved their beers to me and I gave them a polite head nod and continued my run.

Then, something funny happened. I turned the corner of a street and started running up a long hill. My legs were burning, and I figured I'd walk the rest of the way until I got back to a flat surface. What had happened was I had compared myself with the other dads in the neighborhood who were drinking beer, and I felt good about myself. There was no use going through all the pain of attacking that hill; after all, I had favorably compared myself against others. It took away some of my drive during that run.

The following morning, I went to a cool event. It was a multicultural boot camp put on by a local group who were in shape enough to look like NFL players. There were many people there who had reached elite physical levels. Compared to them, I felt unfit. I left there feeling bad about my physical condition. The day before, I lost my drive because I felt great about myself. The next day, I lost my drive because I felt bad about myself. I felt both ways because I compared myself to others.

I learned that the only person you can compare yourself to is you. Are you a little better today than yesterday? Are you slimmer than you were last month? Did you read the book you told yourself you'd read this month? Did you start taking that cooking class you told your friends about?

Most people only like comparing themselves to others when they're doing better than them. They justify their situations, even if they're not ideal, because others are doing worse. "Well, compared to my brother, the one who never graduated college, I'm doing great!" The false justification fools them into feeling good about not living the lives they have the potential to live.

The truth is that no one really knows anyone else's story. In this social-media-crazy age, we only see people's highlights. But we don't know what demons they wrestle with or the hell they've gone through. It's like mentally preparing for a marathon— they only think of the positive parts, hearing the gun go off, turning the corner to cheers, people handing them plastic cups of water and patting them on the back, crossing the finish line with both hands raised. They don't think that in Mile 18, they're going to have a massive leg cramp or that the weather can be unusually warm for that time of year.

I saw a cartoon image of a guy in a helicopter; below it was a guy in a sports car, thinking, *that must be nice.* Next to him was another guy in a clunker, looking at the sports car, thinking, *that must be nice.* Next to him was a guy on a bike, looking at the clunker, thinking, *that must be nice.* Next to him was a guy running to work, looking at the guy on the bike, thinking, *that must be nice.* Next to him was a guy in a wheelchair, watching the guy running, thinking, *that must be nice.*

Instead of trying to keep up with the Joneses and feeling bad about yourself,

celebrate the Joneses and learn from them.

If you asked Mr. and Mrs. Jones, they'd most likely be more than happy to share what they know. Comparing yourself with anyone other than you is foolish because everyone's experience is different. It's never comparing apples to apples.

GIVE YOURSELF GRACE

I'm going to get to the point very quickly on this topic. Ready? Here it goes. You're not perfect. You're going to mess up. Expect it. Given that what I said is an absolute truth, allow yourself forgiveness for your mess-ups! Then, learn from them.

I see people beating themselves all too often in the weight loss world. Someone cheats on his or her diet for one meal, and then gives up. People gain two pounds instead of losing two pounds, and the wheels come off, and the next month, they gain five more.

You'll have bad days. You'll have days that you didn't do better than yesterday. Days you didn't make the phone calls, go to the gym, chose binge-watching on Netflix instead of spending quality time with your loved ones. Let it go. Don't beat yourself up about it.

Love yourself unconditionally. There are parents of serial killers who still love them. There is nothing their children can do, even as adults, that will change the love they have for them. Love yourself like that. It's important. Not to mention, a much happier way to live.

On a scale of one to ten, how much would you say you love yourself? It's not egotistical to say ten. In fact, it's really the only acceptable answer. It doesn't mean you're perfect; it just means that you're open to growing and learning. If your love for yourself is at a four, you'll believe that others can also only love you as a four. Loving yourself means forgiving yourself. There is no love without forgiveness.

Tim Storey told me about a time he was on a plane—a private jet—owned by a very wealthy guy. As they talked, Tim asked him a pretty common question:

"So, are you married or single?"

The guy said he was divorced.

Tim said, "Okay, but that wasn't the question. When did you get divorced?"

The guy told him, "Twenty-three years ago."

Tim told me that he felt bad for the extremely wealthy man who owned a private jet, because the man was stuck in the past.

Tim told me another story about a third-grader who didn't make it to the bathroom in time and pissed in his pants. Everyone in the school referred to him as the kid who pees his pants. In high school, they still referred to him that way. At their twenty-year high school reunion, they referred to him, and remembered him, as the guy who pees his pants.

Sadly, too many people remember the shameful things that others have long forgotten about. They lied so much when they were in high school, they think themselves untrustworthy at forty. Or if they make one bad investment, they consider themselves bad investors and never invest again, losing out on great opportunities. It's silly. As human beings, we grow, we evolve, we learn new things, and we develop new habits.

Open yourself to the possibilities of a great future by forgetting the failures of your past. There's a saying that I couldn't disagree more with: *Ignorance is bliss.* What an ignorant statement! Ignorance is costly. If you're ignorant about something, you can't improve upon it. It means you don't have the information necessary to control the situation. How is that blissful when you're at the mercy of things and people around you? Bliss is having the knowledge and certainty that no matter what comes your way, you're more than capable of handling it. Bliss is knowing that if you fall down, you'll learn and pick yourself up again and not fall from the same thing the next time.

There's another saying that I don't agree with: *Money is the root of all evil.* I would say that ignorance is the root of all evil. Knowledge is power, and knowledge is the opposite of ignorance. I'll take it one step further. I believe knowledge is only potential power. Knowledge only becomes powerful when you take action.

Sadly, many good-intentioned people don't know how to put themselves first. They have such big hearts that they put others ahead of them—their spouses, their children, their churches, their communities, non-profits, stray dogs, etc. But I'm here to tell you that although your heart is good, it's in the wrong place. You need to put You first!

Imagine that life is like a burning ship. If you don't have the strength, speed, and resilience to help yourself out, there's no way you can help others and keep them from drowning. Other people's welfare, including your family members, are their responsibilities. Naturally, I'm not saying to kick your ten-year-old daughter out to the streets. I'm telling you that the better you take care of yourself, the better equipped you'll be—financially, emotionally, physically—to take care of others. Love others, yes, but not at the risk of not loving yourself.

ACTION STEPS:

Create your champions list:

Who do you know that can mentor you?

Who do you not know that can mentor you?

What have you not forgiven yourself about?

How has that held you back?

6

HABITUAL PRISONERS

Habit is stronger than reason.

— *GEORGE SANTAYANA*

CREATURES OF HABIT

You are your habits, and if you don't pay attention, you will become prisoner to them. Chances are, whatever you do moment to moment and day to day is not the first time you did it. If you took a particular route to work yesterday, it's because you've done it before, many times, and now, you do it automatically. If you tucked your shirt into your pants, it's because you've done it before. In fact, what you did yesterday has more say on what you'll do today than what you want to do.

Changing your life is impossible without changing your habits. Many times, people try to emulate other people's morning routines (habits), which is a good place to start if it's someone who is where you want to be. However, we all have our own idiosyncrasies. Be you. The only thing to find out what you like or not is to experience them and stick to the good ones that suit your senses and surroundings. For example, just because a billionaire wakes up and cranks up motivational music every morning doesn't mean that you should do the same. The point is to experience it, pay attention, and make a decision as to whether it's right for you.

I like to set myself up for success, so it starts the night before. Prior to going to bed, I set my alarm in another room. This forces me out of bed instead of hitting snooze three times and wasting forty-five minutes. The alarm is not a blaring sound; who likes that noise? I set my alarm to play my favorite music. I preprogram my coffee machine. I love waking up to the smell of freshly brewed coffee. I lay out the clothes I'm going to wear the next day: shoes, socks in the shoes, shorts, and shirt.

When I open my eyes to music I like, I condition myself to jump out of bed with excitement. I create a habit of asking, first thing: *what am I excited about today?*

By the time I shut off the music-alarm, I can smell the coffee, and I know what I'm excited about. As I drink my first drink of water of the day, I condition myself to be present in the moment and to be grateful for another day. Unlike the vast majority of people more than fourteen years of age, I don't lie in bed and reach over for my phone first thing. In fact, I have made it a habit of not looking at my phone for at least thirty minutes after I've woken up. (I learned this from Ed Mylett.) I can't risk the beginning of a great day to things outside of my control. In fact, my entire morning and evening routine is made up of a collection of habits I developed after listening to what others have done.

The Pareto Principle (also known as the 80/20 Rule) states that roughly 80 percent of outcomes come from 20 percent of causes. In other words, 80 percent of the business comes from 20 percent of your clients. Eighty percent of the beer consumed is by 20 percent of the beer drinkers. If you do the right things habitually, meaning you've changed some of your bad habits and created new, better habits, it's okay if you mess up 20 percent of the time. If it's the other way around, there's a 100-percent certainty that you won't get what you want out of life.

I certainly don't feel like working out every morning. But since I've created a habit of what I'm excited about, and my health is part of that and what I'm grateful for, and the places and stages I envision myself standing on, it pulls me to work out, like a boat pulls a water skier. Once I drink water and start stretching, and I'm grateful and excited—I'm ready to work out! I have purpose. I'm driven. *Where dem weights at?*

I have found that mornings are not good times to make big decisions. So, the night before, I tell myself, out loud, what I'm going to do in the morning. When the morning comes, I hold myself accountable to what I told myself. I challenge you to do the same thing. It's a mental habit that has to be developed.

Changing your habits changes your being-ness. Others notice, and it affects their belief about who you are to them. At one point, I frequented a bowling alley in the city where I live. Every time I'd go, I'd order the same beer. It became so frequent that the waitress would greet me with that beer in hand. When I made a commitment to myself to get in better shape and build muscle, beer-drinking was not part of the plan. When I went to the bowling alley, the waitress told me she'd get my beer as she walked by. I told her I'd have water. She paused and said, "What? Like, for now? Sure. Let me know when you're ready for the beer." It took some time, but now she hands me the water with the same smile she handed me the beer.

This may be one of the reasons you are afraid to change yourself —it not only affects you, but it also affects the people in your life who have made a decision about who you are.

HABITS

The definition of a habit is: *a settled or regular tendency or practice, especially one that is hard to give up.* Giving up a habit is incredibly difficult. That's why I'm not asking you to give up any of your habits; I'm asking you to replace them!

Habits are what you do automatically, when you're on cruise control. You may think, *but I've been doing this for twenty years; I don't have the discipline to do something different the next twenty years!* I've got good news for you: it only takes thirty days to create a new habit and replace a bad one.

You don't need to be disciplined forever. You only need to be intentional on doing something better for one month.

Then, that new thing will become the normal thing you do when you're on cruise control.

We all have habitual thought processes which play into the four stressors—physical (our bodies), chemical (what we eat and drink), mental (our thoughts), and emotional (our feelings). The mental and emotional ones tend to be the hardest to replace. Try replacing counter-productive mental thoughts and unhealthy ways of feeling about yourself with something better. This is the driver that will change your life. Know this: each and every habit, including the ones you've done for as long as you can remember, can be replaced. If you've written down the habits that don't serve you, as I asked in a previous chapter, just think: in thirty days, you could replace it. How exciting is that?

It's time to un-stick your future and change some of the current habits that have paralyzed your progress. There are people who are known more for their habits, or for what has happened to them, than for their names. Some women in circles are known as "the woman whose husband left her," or "the woman whose daughter was tragically killed." That's because the woman has allowed negative, woe-is-me habits to become so distinct, she is now identified by them. They have allowed bad things to become their being-ness. Their words are habitually depressing. Their worlds are always sad. They dress in drab colors. It's almost as if they are constantly seeking attention or fishing for people to cheer them up. Their thoughts are stuck on victimhood, and their emotions are stuck on pity.

Mental and emotional habits are the difference between seeing hope in something or dismay, faith or fear, winning or losing, loving your life or wishing you could be someone else.

STACK

The best way to create good habits to replace bad habits is to Stack 'em. Allow me to explain. Stack up bad emotions with bad habits. If you have a drinking problem, stack up the negative things that come with it:

- Suffering with a hangover
- Saying something stupid and regretting it
- Embarrassing yourself
- Gaining weight
- Sleeping later
- Not being as productive as you could be
- Getting arrested for drunk driving, or worse, causing a fatal accident

Then, stack up the pleasure of replacing booze with water:

- Being better-hydrated
- Losing weight

- Being more alert
- Being more productive
- Waking up better
- Being more responsible
- Being in better health
- Being less angry, resulting in better relationships

Let's say that there's an event in six months, and you want to be fitter, slimmer, and sexier. Stack all the pain that comes with doing nothing, and imagine how you will feel at the party: less confident, sluggish, wishing you were invisible. Stack up the pleasure you'll feel if you reach your goal: the clothes you'll wear, the strut, the confidence, the feeling you'll have when you get back to your hotel room that you made an impression on people.

I recently completed something I had on my Vision Board for five years. I participated at the St. Louis Cardinals Fantasy Camp. It's a camp, run by the Cardinals, for people like me who love the game of baseball and wished we pursued our dream to play in the major leagues. Well, for five glorious days, we can!

The first day, you "try out," meaning they take you through workouts and tryouts, and then they select the teams. Then, you play the games. Your coaches are no less than Cardinal legends! Then, there are the playoffs; it gets very competitive.

I wanted to make sure I would represent myself well, so, six months prior to the camp, I made the decision that I would get in shape (the same decision that didn't allow me to have drinks, even when I went bowling). I replaced old, non- or anti-health related habits with strength and conditioning routines. I went to the Cardinals Fantasy Camp feeling fit and strong, which gave me confidence.

While there, I played all-out. Not just in the games, but in the camaraderie, in speaking with baseball legends and hearing their stories, in learning the nuances of baseball—all of it. I made the choice to be present wherever I was and in whatever I was doing. The fantasy camp had been on my Vision Board for five years, and I wanted to experience as much of it as I could. My decision to replace some habits for healthier ones paid off in more ways than one. At the end of it all, my team won the "World Series!"

YOU DON'T KNOW WHAT YOU DON'T KNOW

Many people think they are someone they are not. My friend, Eli, learned this the hard way. He was transitioning from twenty-two years in corporate life to go on his own as a freelance writer. He hired a life coach to help him through the transition. The first day, his coach asked him what the four most important things to him were. Eli answered, "My faith, my family, my health, my finances."

The coach sent Eli an Excel spreadsheet and told him to fill it out. Whatever he did most in each half hour, from the time he woke up to the time he went to bed, he was to jot down on the sheet. This way, the coach could get a snapshot of Eli's life in just one week and would be better suited to serve him. Eli dutifully filled out what he did for the better part of each half hour and emailed it to his coach. When they met again, Eli had no idea what awaited him.

"Why did you lie to me?" the coach asked.

Eli told me that he was embarrassed and annoyed at the accusation. After all, why hire a life coach to hide his life from him? "I didn't lie about anything," Eli explained. "Everything I did for the majority of each half hour is accurately written on the sheet."

The coach nodded in agreement. "I believe you that this is how you lived the last seven days, but I'm not saying you lied as you filled out the form. My question is, why did you lie to me when you told me the four most important things in your life are your faith, family, health, and finances?"

"What do you mean?" Eli asked, clearly confused.

"Based on what you do, the television is the most important thing in your life. In fact, outside of church, you didn't spend any time on your faith. You also didn't schedule time for your wife or kids."

Eli was still hurt, but even more embarrassed. He thought he was living a life that he wasn't living!

"I actually don't think you lied to me, though," his coach continued with the lesson. "I think you told me what you thought was the truth, but the reality is that you've been lying to yourself as to who you are."

Today, Eli aligns his values with how he spends his time—his habits. He is a very successful writer and businessman. In order to find ultimate success in anything, it's easier if your values and the habits that take up your day are in alignment. I also recommend having a mentor or coach who will be able to see things differently from you.

ACTION STEPS:

Are you who you tell yourself you are?

What is one habit that you've longed to implement?

Why have you not done so?

Is that a reason, or an excuse?

What good emotions can you STACK to implement that habit?

When (exact date) will you replace a bad habit with a good one?

Promise yourself that you'll do this for thirty days until you get over the uncomfortable-ness of doing it and it becomes a habit:

I, _____, promise to implement this habit for thirty days, beginning (date) _____.

7
VISION AND IMAGINATION

Logic will get you from A to B.

Imagination will take you everywhere.

— *ALBERT EINSTEIN*

FORESIGHT

The word "vision" has many definitions, but I am speaking about the ability to think about or plan the future with imagination or wisdom. Vision is using your imagination to create a new version of the future for yourself that currently doesn't exist.

A derivative of having vision also means to have foresight—that's to be able to know what's going to happen before it happens or to know of something before anyone else. I also call this "intuition" or a "gut feeling." Some of the most successful business owners on the planet have tremendous foresight. They can see when an industry or product is about to explode or go into a recession. Their wealth isn't made in knowing that, though; it's made in knowing that and capitalizing on the competitive edge by taking action. How do they know? From experience and learning from mistakes.

My version of vision, or foresight, is to identify or see something in the future that has not physically happened or been created yet. In the context of this book, and what I want to impart to you, is this: you have a superpower in that you can create the future vision of the ideal situation or life you want to create. The superpower takes four steps to manifest:

1. See it in the future as if it were your present
2. Write it down
3. Believe it
4. Take action

Do something, even if it's a little something, every day to make it happen.

Having a clearly defined vision of the future is like having a steering wheel on a ship; without it, you'll be blown around by the wind and the waves and live a life of uncertainty. Your engines could work fine, but you'll never know where you're going to end up.

We can't stop time, and the future is going to happen. If you are still alive, you're going to be living somewhere, doing something to earn a living, buying things, doing things, having relationships...well, you get the point.

Only by having a clear vision today of how you want your life to be in the future will you have the best shot at getting there. It amazes me that people are so frustrated with their current realities. They'll bitch and complain about it, blaming the government, their upbringing, or anything else that foolishly makes them feel better about themselves in the moment, instead of taking responsibility for where they are in life. They'll complain that they don't have money to take their families on yearly vacations or that they need to pay for medicines because of their health issues, yet they'll do nothing to alter the trajectory of their lives. Five years later, they'll have the same complaints with the same lives. That is no way to live, my friend.

Most people overestimate what they can do in a year and underestimate what they can do in a lifetime. People also have a tendency to overthink things and make them more complicated than they really are.

The principles of life are pretty simple. Figure out what your purpose is in life. Be patient in the results as you learn and experience things. Pay attention to what resonates with you and what doesn't.

Create a compelling and clear vision of the life you want to build.

Visualize and meditate on this life until it becomes real to you, before it is a physical reality. Have faith and believe it will happen. Take action every day toward this life. Repeat.

ACT LIKE A CHILD

Children live in the imaginative state. They have not "downloaded" a bunch of beliefs or limitations on what's possible in their lives. They only think in terms of what is possible by using their imaginations. Most adults have unlearned this skill. We tend to project what we believe, based on our previous experiences in life, into what we think is possible. This is living in the past. If you live in the past, your future will look very similar to your past.

When this happens, I like to play the "what if" game. What if there were no limitations? What if money were no issue? What if I had the time? What if I allowed my visions to flow through me without justifying them? What would be possible then?

Simply put, leave all options open and constantly ask questions of what is possible. If you are aware of this, you will start to pick up on all of the times you limit yourself.

ASSETS AND LIABILITIES

Sometimes, when I am speaking at universities or entrepreneur seminars, I like to have everyone do an activity to discover what they really think about themselves. I do this activity myself on a regular basis to remind me of how amazing I truly am (and I say that with humility).

As you know, the world is a tough place and has a tendency to focus on the negative. Human beings pick up this habit pretty quickly because it is everywhere in our culture. This is a great example of the law of familiarity and the power of proximity. The more you are around something, the easier it is to accept and adapt to it.

What you believe about yourself matters more than you know, and if you aren't aware of what you believe about yourself, then nothing will change. With most habits, the first step is to become aware, and there is a simple task to become aware of what you think of yourself.

This process came from something that happened to me when I was twenty-one years old. At that time, I believed I was not important, I was inferior to others, and I was terrified that no one liked me. I had the classic case of low self-esteem, and because of it, I lived in constant fear of not fitting in, rejection, and ridicule. One night, I met someone who changed my life.

After a few hours of amazing conversation during which I was asked about my life, views, talents, strengths, weaknesses, family, and future plans, a woman asked me a simple question.

"So, what's your catch?"

I asked, "What do you mean, 'what's my catch?'"

She said, "You're twenty-one years old; in grad school to be a doctor; you sing and play guitar; you've played college baseball, so you're an athlete; and to boot, you're good-looking and a nice guy. What? Are you perfect?"

"Ummm, I live with my grandma?"

"That's adorable!"

What she had brought to my attention was a list of all of my assets, things I had taken for granted about myself. I didn't value myself, so I had never considered that others could look up to me or even value me until she gave me compelling reasons why I was a good person with a bright future. As it turns out this woman became my wife within a year. It was around then that I started a new habit, which I will ask you to do before we go on to the next chapter. Grab a sheet of paper, and on the left side, write all of your assets. Write down all of the things that are great about you, all of the things that make you an amazing person who deserves an amazing life on your terms. On the right side of the paper, write down all of your liabilities—all of the things that you say about yourself that are negative, all the things you don't like about yourself, and all of your insecurities.

Do not move on to the next part until you have completed this task. Take five minutes to complete this. *Yes, it is that important.*

When I teach this to a group in-person, I almost always have to tell the people to stop writing down their liabilities; they generally have short lists of assets.

How about you? Did you have a bigger list of liabilities than assets? Most people do. I want you to understand this very important truth: this is what you are thinking about yourself every second of your life. It's hard for most people to make a long list of assets because we are taught to focus on the negatives, and if you remember what I said before, *like* attracts *like*; what you focus on expands.

If you constantly think more negative thoughts about yourself than positive, then you will get more negative results. So, take time to pick up this new habit of identifying what you say about yourself to yourself, make sure your asset list gets longer and longer while your liability list shrinks over time, and make sure you repeat it enough times until it becomes real to you.

If you really want to take this to the next level, ask the people who are closest to you what they believe your assets and liabilities are. You will be surprised about how well people know you. Don't react to what they are saying, either. It will be uncomfortable, but you should come into this task with childlike wonder and imagination and gratitude that these people love you enough to take the time to be honest with you. Gratitude and appreciation is the emotion you want to experience and the emotion you want these people to feel from you.

ACTION STEPS:

What did you learn about yourself?

How do you feel after making your list?

What steps will you take to make your list asset-heavy?

8
WHO ARE YOU?

"Be yourself, but always your better self!"

— *KARL MAESER*

KNOW THYSELF

Who you are today is the compilation of all your decisions, habits, and patterns you've developed. They have heavily influenced the world around you and the perspective in which you see things, your point of view. In your subconscious, you've developed a grading system on almost everything; it's like a *this equals that*, pre-framed thought pattern that's so integral, it makes assumptions for you without you consciously having to think about it.

You may not be who you want to be, which is most likely why you're reading this book, but who you are at this very moment is who you've thought you were. If you're not happy with where you are with the five main pillars of life—Relationships, Health, Faith, Finances, and Career, you can still change. Who you *are* doesn't have to be who you *will be* for the rest of your life. The first step to that is visualizing who it is you want to be.

For example, if you can visualize yourself as a millionaire, what do you need to believe in order for that to happen? You'd have to believe that you deserve to hang out with millionaires. You'd have to believe that you can start mimicking much of what they do. You'd have to believe that you have the skills or talent or education or experience to obtain it. You'd have to believe that life happens *for* you, not *to* you. You'd have to believe that you need to hang out with millionaires. You'd have to believe that you would start mimicking much of what they do.

I love to speak at colleges. I love to see a sea of bright, young faces, most of who feel they have life all figured out, even though any of them rarely do. During my talk, I'll have them think about their ideal partners. That question usually brings its own energy into the room as some of the kids look around while others get embarrassed to just think about it. Sometimes, I feel they slip into a Middle School mentality.

Once the buzz dies down, I ask them to write down the person they'd love to be with—looks, body, hair, money, title, car, hobbies, etc. I tell them not to qualify themselves and just let their imaginations take shape on the type of person they would most like to be with.

Then I ask the million-dollar question: "Who do you have to become to attract that person?"

They all stop writing and smiling.

I usually repeat the question, and then add this one: "Would that person want you right now?" Some of the kids give me a look of dismay or defeat.

I repeat, "Who do you have to become to attract that person?"

The ones who start writing again, I believe, are the only ones who can attract that which they most desire. I remind them, butterflies aren't born butterflies. The person you'd love to be with, to you, is a butterfly, yet, you're a caterpillar. If you want that person, get in your cocoon and become the butterfly that he or she is looking for.

Most people who are not financially rich believe that it's too hard to be rich. Grant Cardone has a great response to that; he says, "It's harder being poor!" Hard is not knowing if you can pay next month's rent. Hard is not being able to buy your child a decent birthday present. Hard is not having a vehicle and being dependent on public transportation or rides from friends and family. Hard is not being able to provide decent health coverage for your sick mother, spouse, or child.

The road to your success in the five pillars has already been paved. You don't have to cut down any trees, blast any mountains to flatten the surfaces, or lay down any concrete. Success leaves clues. Honestly, all you really have to do is want it so bad that you do what needs to be done to get it. That's it!

You need to beware the two major roadblocks:

1. You'll have to fight your brain. At times, you'll feel like you're fighting every fiber of your being. That's what your brain wants you to think, but it's a "little white lie." Your brain wants you to travel down the path of least resistance. It'll tell you to celebrate a Tuesday and get drunk so that you don't wake up ready to hit the gym in the morning. It'll tell you that you deserve a comfortable life (which is the life you're living now).
2. You also have to fight the character you've created. Those closest to you have made decisions about who

you are and what you can or can't do. When they see you starting to change, they'll tell you, as a friend—as someone who cares about you, that you shouldn't do this new thing.

- *You don't know the first thing about owning a business.*
- *She is too out-of-your-league; you're going to end up being hurt.*
- *I think you can do it, but I don't think now is the right time.*
- *Shouldn't you get more training first?*
- *You're crazy to pay a coach that much!*

When you disrupt the box they put you into, you challenge their own comfort zones, and they'd rather try to talk you out of it than look inward and challenge themselves to at least try to live the lives of their own design.

Just remember: people cannot see your dreams, and most people have given up on theirs. So, when someone starts telling you why you can't do something that you feel compelled to do, they are only projecting their beliefs and their fears on you. It has nothing to do with you, your dream, or the possibility of that dream coming true.

You can't get healthier by eating the same things, not going to the gym, and binge-eating sweets. Change requires change. You're going to have to give things up that you like. You may love banana splits on Friday nights or gambling every other week with friends or sleeping in on weekends. The truth is that your habits are your habits because you enjoy doing them. You may regret the hangover, but you like the buzz. Most people see improvements as only positive, but the truth is that improvements oftentimes require loss. Remember though, to be that better you, whatever you're losing is worth it.

DEFEAT THE "HOW"

If you knew how to live the life of your dreams, you'd have done it already. The problem is that you can dream it, and you can be inspired to take action, but you don't know how to do it. Stop asking "how." Get the *how* out of your way.

Just focus on what you want—the outcome you want. The *how* will reveal itself, most likely in ways you would have never dreamed of. God's rule is to seek and you will find, to knock and the doors will open. He doesn't tell you *what* to seek. He doesn't give you the speakeasy secret password for the door to open. If you can stay consistently focused on *what* you want, *how* you get it will happen. You just have to meet God halfway.

It's okay not to know how you'll meet the person of your dreams, or how you'll become a household name, or how you'll lose the thirty pounds and keep them off, or how to start a seven-figure business. The ironic thing is that you don't need to know how.

Accept that you don't know how. It's fine. Someone at some point in history figured out how to achieve the thing(s) you want. He or she has probably written it down in a book. There are probably tons of videos about it on YouTube. There are potential mentors who would love to help you with the *how*. Hang out with them. Befriend them. Hire them, if you have to. Walk how they walk. Talk like they talk. See how they handle phone calls, adversity, victories, and partnerships. Find out whom they turn to for help, the books they have read, what excites them, and why they are so persistent.

The How is a Confusion Beast. It opens the mental and emotional doorway to bloodsuckers called Impossible and Unreasonable. Focusing on *how* starts to limit the wondrous power of faith, God, the universe, magic, and manifestation.

Rome wasn't built in a day. Remember, you don't have to live your dream life overnight. All you have to do is replace one habit at a time, consistently, over time.

Be obsessed with the life you want to live. Talk about it, dream about it, think about it, pray about it, and work toward it. The more time, energy, and effort you put toward it, the more likely it will come true.

Let's say you have an hour to get a project done. The more you focus on the project, the more likely you'll complete it within the hour. The more distractions you focus on, such as the time clicking by, and the more you allow doubt and fear to creep in, the less likely it is that you'll complete it. It's the same with your life in terms of days, weeks, months, and years. The more time you devote to distractions, worrying if things won't work out or how they can't work out, the less likely it is that you'll reach your goals.

If you just focus on what you want, and do even the little things that get you an inch closer, you create momentum, and that, my friend, is a powerful ally. Momentum = mass x velocity. The faster an object moves, the harder it is to stop. John Maxwell calls it "The Law of Big Mo." As you start replacing a bad habit (gaining mass), in a quick and efficient manner (gaining velocity) and do it consistently (taking action), you can build up enough momentum that can get you through the toughest of times. Take a train, for example: just one brick can stop it from starting its journey. But once it has gained momentum and reaches top speed, it can smash through an entire brick wall.

Objectively, I can say I've been a successful businessman for most of my adult life—decades. But it was only four short years ago that I did some honest, no-bullshit soul-searching and decided how I wanted the rest of my life to play out. In those few years, I've been in rooms with my role models. I've sat at the feet of masters. The growth I've experienced personally, emotionally, financially, and physically have been nothing short of astounding to me. I didn't know how I would get to where I am, but I got here. I'm not sure how I'm going to get to where I am going to be, but I believe that I'll get there. When doubt tries to creep in, I ask myself a question that puts doubt and fear back in the basement of my subconscious: what am I capable of?

ACTION STEPS:

Who are you today? (Be honest. Relationships: are you a great, good, indifferent, bad, honest, loyal spouse/girlfriend/boyfriend? Do you love your career? Do you have the money you'd like to have?) Who are you?

Who do you want to be?

When will you make the commitment to become that person mentally and emotionally?

Date: _____

When will you take your first action?

Date: _____

9
TIME TRAVEL

"As you think, so you become. "

— BRUCE LEE

DR. G'S SAYINGS TO LIVE BY

Faith is the substance of things hoped for and the evidence of things not seen Hebrews 11:1

You have not because you asked not James. 4: 2-3

He who loves to sleep and the folding of hands, poverty will set upon you like a thief in the night. Proverbs 24:33

You must write the vision and make it plain so that he who reads it will run to it and even though it may tarry, wait for it and it will come in appointment to time Habbukuk. 2:2-4

Be still and know that I am God Psalm. 46:10

Ask and it will be given to you; seek and you will find; knock and the door will be opened to you. Matthew 7:7

Again, truly I tell you that if two of you on earth agree about anything they ask for, it will be done for them by my Father in heaven Matthew. 18:19

He who works his land shall have abundance, he who chases fantasy lacks wisdom.

For as a man thinks in his heart, so is he Proverbs 23:7

YOUR BELIEFS

We are who we are, we believe what we believe, and we react how we react based on our past experiences. As I mentioned in this book, your habits have more to do with what you do today than what you want to do. But habits are not the main topic in this chapter. I want you to explore the precursor to habits: your beliefs.

Your belief in God, humanity, the opposite sex, money, yourself, and everything else comes from the collection of your experiences. Today, your mind calculates assumptions, stereotypes, judgments, and biases before you can even think about them. Your past is like a mini supercomputer that shares data with your brain faster than you can even decide on something. If you're not where you want to be or not even on the road to take you to where you want to be, it's time to travel back in time and assess the information guiding you throughout your life.

Making decisions today as you would when you were five, ten, or twenty years old usually doesn't work out well when you're in your thirties or older. However, you make decisions for your future that aren't going to work out because you've not traveled back in your memories or challenged if the assumptions or beliefs you made years ago are still your beliefs now. This is why many people say stupid things like:

"Rich people are greedy and mean."
"Poor people can't be trusted."
"White people are racist."
"Fat people are lazy."
"Men are jerks."
"Women are gold-diggers."
"Weight loss is hard."
"I am never good enough."
"I am not worthy of love."

And on and on it goes.

At some point, you had an experience, your body took in the information, and you made a conclusion which is now your belief, that you accept, and take in as truth.

Travel through your memories and try to find out when you came to such conclusions about how you think of others and how you think of yourself.

When I speak at a conference, dive deep with someone, or coach, I hear people blaming others—their parents, their upbringing, or their lack of resources. As an adult, I think if you were to time-travel, you'd see that your parents were doing their best with what they had. If you're a parent, you've realized that your children did not come with manuals. If you have more than one child, they're probably opposites in personality, so to reach them effectively, you need to act and react differently toward them.

No parent has all the correct answers. Many children of wealthy parents lose their money and end up broke. Many children of poor parents make their own way and wind up rich. Christian parents have children who turn their backs on their religion. Atheist parents have children who find and believe in faith. We as parents don't have the answers, yet many people would prefer to blame their parents instead of taking responsibility for their experiences and the beliefs they have created.

Beliefs are often tied to emotion. Don't get me wrong; emotions are necessary. They are proof that you're alive. They are there to protect and guide you, but if you let your emotions run your life, the path to your best self and potential future will elude you. Use your feelings; don't let them use you. Ask yourself: *Why do I feel a certain way about certain things? Why did I blow my lid? Why was I so blissful?* Start analyzing why you feel certain emotions based on where you are, who you're with, and what's happening. You will be able to intentionally put yourself in situations that make you feel good and get out of situations you know will make you feel bad. This is one of the most simple life hacks; it can work wonders for you, but it will only work for you if you work it.

You can't change the past; yet, you can change your association with it and the beliefs that came from it. Hence, time-travel. Go. Now. You don't have to wait for an invitation from Elon Musk, your government, your spouse, or your parents. If you analyze it, this is the foundation of what psychologists do; they ask you to time-travel through your memories.

If you do it and you're honest with yourself, you could very well conclude that you've been operating based on wrong information. I always thought credit cards were bad because my dad said it repeatedly. I realized, though, that they're beneficial if I'm disciplined enough and use them properly. It was getting into $20,000 worth of credit debt by going to the 10X Growth Conference in 2019 that changed my life to the point where now I'm writing this book. Had I kept my father's belief in credit cards, my business could still be struggling, I'd be a lot unhealthier, and I'd be frustrated.

By time-traveling and inputting accurate, sober information into your thought-making process, you'll have more control of your life and be more confident about your actions. When you feel more certain—the opposite of which is uncertainty, which drives people to panic—you live a better life.

There are only two things that are keeping you where you are: information and habits. New information will lead to new beliefs and new beliefs will lead to new habits.

NEUTRAL THINKING

In cars from the previous generation, and maybe even in some new cars today, the gear shift went in this order: Park, Drive, Neutral, Reverse, and then a Reverse Low or a Drive Low (for when the vehicle had a lot of weight). I mention this to point out that when you're in Reverse, you don't go straight to Drive; you must pass the gearshift through neutral first. When it comes to ways of thinking, sometimes it's difficult to go from Negative (Reverse) thinking to Positive (Drive) thinking, especially when trying to replace bad habits of thought.

For instance, if you've never been able to lose weight and keep it off, the Negative thinking would be: *I can't lose weight and keep it off.* Based on the evidence and your personal history, that may be a more believable statement than a Positive thought such as *I can lose weight and keep it off.* A Neutral view is: *although I haven't been able to lose weight and keep it off, it is possible.*

I like to say a neutral view is a third-party view, without emotion, just pointing out the facts. If you start thinking and believing it's possible, you're not trying to believe a lie, so your subconscious mind can champion that thought. Eventually, knowing that it's possible, you can change the thought from Neutral to Positive: *this time, I'm going to lose weight and keep it off.*

If you can identify negative thoughts and bring them to a neutral thought, it will then be easier to turn them into positive thought patterns that will eventually result in positive actions that will benefit you in the long run.

Replacing thoughts in your head takes time, just as changing your body from unfit to fit takes time. It takes continual, intentional thinking, just like it takes continual, intentional trips to the gym. It's a slow, steady process, but one well worth the journey.

People say, "Oh, I'm such an idiot!"

Is that true?

"Well, not all the time."

Then how about saying, "The history of me in this area is not good, but I can study or practice at it and become good."

That is Neutral Thinking. It's almost like a third party steps into your brain and takes the emotion out of the topic by taking out any negative or positive feelings attached to it. Or it's as if you're giving someone else advice, except it's for you. If you remove all of the emotional filters around something, you'll get to the reality of the situation.

I learned this concept from the book, *It Takes What It Takes* by Trevor Moawad and Andy Staples. I highly recommend reading it to become a neutral thinker first.

DEATH IS A GREAT TEACHER

We get so caught up in moments that oftentimes we forget; moments are fleeting. Our lives are fleeting. There will be a day when the earth continues, but we will no longer be. It's cliché but true; we aren't guaranteed tomorrow. Death is a fact of life.

When I think about the day I will no longer be here, I don't focus on it; I focus on today, the present. Knowing that I won't be here motivates me to make sure I do something I'm proud of today. I hope you think the same as you read this part of the book. Most likely, you're not going to be remembered 100-200 years from now, and that's okay.

Stop thinking so much of what others might think or say about you and allowing it to stop you from being who you have the potential to be.

Live your life instead of living someone else's version of your life.

Tony Robbins talks about The Rocking Chair Test. He says, and I'm paraphrasing here, when you're ninety years old and your speed, athleticism, energy, and drive are gone and you're in a rocking chair, what do you want to be thinking? Will your thoughts be full of wishes? *I wish I went skydiving. I wish I had left that terrible relationship. I wish I had stuck to my weight loss plan. I wish I had opened my own business. I wish I had called and apologized. I wish I had the courage to stand up for myself more. I wish I tried the Comedy Open Mic Night at least one time. I wish I had learned to play the piano. I wish I didn't stay home almost every night watching TV for hours. I wish I had gone on that cruise. I wish I would have experienced more of life. I wish I would have written that book* (this was me for a while).

Life is all about experiences. When it's all said and done, do you want to wish you had done things and sit in that rocking chair full of regret, or would you rather reminisce on the memories of taking action and doing the things you desired? Do you want to be in regret or remembrance? It's going to be one or the other, and only you can choose—not by thought or words, but by action.

When that time comes for me, I will remember how I worked to turn my mentors and role models into my peers. I will remember going on the dream vacation with my wife, not *wishing* we had gone on it. I'm going to remember my experiences, not wish I had them. I will fondly remember getting in shape, paying money, and going to Fantasy Camp with the Cardinals. I will remember the many stages I was blessed to speak on. I will remember millions of faces looking at me as I brought a message of positivity and hope. I don't want to have regrets. Regrets suck. Like Jim Rohn said, "If you think the price of action is a lot, wait until you get the bill for regret."

One of the reasons why I wrote this book is because there's a chance I won't get to meet you. However, I believe I have a message that can help you. I want to rock in that rocking chair and imagine the people who read this book and recollect the lovely compliments I received because I served them when I had the chance.

Death doesn't scare me; it motivates me. I think of the day I'm in a casket, and I realize that whatever they say about me then is up to how I live my life now. Sure, it saddens me to think that the people who love me would be mourning and crying. But then, I think of what people will say about me to my kids. That I was an okay doctor? That I was a nice guy? That's just not enough for me. I want my kids to hear how I inspired people, motivated them, and made their lives better. The only way to do that is by becoming the type of person who could make people say those words.

Become the person you're meant to be without limitations while you have the time. Think about the Rocking Chair Test whenever you are afraid of challenging your comfort zone and doing something new. Remember, it's what you do now that people will talk about when you're gone. Why not have them talk about your greatness? Then, maybe, if it is your destiny, people will still be talking about you a hundred years from now.

ACTION STEPS:

What decisions have you made in the past about relationships, money, career, health, and faith that need to be revisited?

What other perspectives could there be about these areas?

What beliefs do you have that are negative and keep you in a negative cycle?

Write down neutral-thinking statements about these thoughts.

Take the Rocking Chair Test. Imagine yourself at ninety years old and in a rocking chair.

What are some things that you "wish" you had done?

10

ONLY YOU CAN SAVE YOU

What we achieve inwardly will change outer reality.

— *GREEK PHILOSOPHER PLUTARCH*

YOU GET WHAT YOU DESERVE

Forgive me for the next few paragraphs if I'm not grammatically correct and capitalize the word Life, as if it were a person, but I don't think most people have a realistic comprehension of what it is. We all go through this unique journey we call Life. But I'd like to use the word Life in the context of someone or something to have a relationship with—a living, breathing, and thinking entity. I know it sounds odd, but maybe only because you've never heard of it said like this before.

As with most relationships, there are expectations, some of which are realistic and others that are unrealistic. An unrealistic relationship with Life is one in which people think they will get what they want—if you believe it, it will come. They will quote you karma-based sayings, such as, "What goes around comes around."

I don't believe what goes around comes around. That puts me at the whim of things outside of my intentions, goals, and control. People who subscribe to that mentality are those who, when things happen, they happen *to* them. I have a better relationship with Life than to believe that.

I believe I am a powerful, creative being, and I put what I want out to the universe, so I believe that when things happen, they don't happen to me; they happen for me.

They happen because the energies I've released from my mind, words, and actions have orchestrated things to happen to advance what I want. They happen so that I can either get closer to what I want or so that I can learn from it, so the next time, I can get closer to what I want.

People with an unhealthy relationship with Life will also tell you that you get what you want out of it. Again, I don't subscribe to that theory. You can want a Lamborghini, you can want six-pack abs, you can want a house on the beach, and you can want to live in Australia—but if you don't make enough money, you won't get the Lamborghini. You won't get six-pack abs if you don't hit the gym consistently and eat healthy foods. If you don't have enough money or good enough credit or don't work with a realtor to help you find the right house, you won't get a place on the beach. And if you live in the States and never go to Australia, you'll never live in Australia.

In short, you don't get what you want out of Life, but Life will get you what you deserve. Life will get you the health you want, the money you want, and the career you're willing to work for, but ONLY IF you deserve it. Life will get you the type of person you want to be in a relationship with, but only if you work to become the type of person that the kind of person you want would be attracted to.

Life is not evil, good, malicious, treacherous, loving, or hateful. Life is a cosmic balance. It is more of a 3-D, multi-dimensional mirror that will take the energy and focus you expend and exchange it for the equivalent of what Life provides. It's lunacy to sow for an apple tree and expect an oak tree. Stop complaining about the "lemons" Life has given you; you've planted for them! People complain about their bad, untrustworthy friends but will not accept the bad, untrustworthy things they've done to others. If you treat Life well, meaning if you go after the relationship with it that you desire, you will have a wonderful relationship with Life.

NO ONE IS COMING TO SAVE YOU

A friend once told me that his uncle told him, "I expected to win the lottery, or to meet a rich lady, or make best friends with a millionaire, you know, that something would happen and I would be all set. But none of those things ever happened. Now that I'm old, I wish I could do so many things over again." It was sad to hear. Even more unfortunate, though, is that, while most people won't openly admit it, they feel that a savior will swoop into their lives and give them the lives of their dreams.

Let me be as clear as I can: no one is coming to save you. No one can force you to get up early and exercise. No one will be with you 24/7 to smack the doughnut out of your hand. No one can make you excel at your job. No one can force you to start your own business and work it for twelve-hour days until it makes you wealthy. Everyone is going through his or her own set of challenges and problems. It's up to you to save yourself.

Most people will not help you until you can reciprocate in some way, shape, or form. They will help you when you can give back or contribute. They will add value to you when and if you can add value to them. That's why the rich get richer. They hang out with rich people, get rich-people information, and work on getting richer.

The reality is that we are all, at our core, selfish. I'm not saying that there aren't amazing people who would give you the shirts off their backs or amazing, giving organizations that will help people when they're down. I am saying, though, that even the people who serve in organizations like that do it from a perspective that it makes them feel good to help the less fortunate. So, in that sense, while people are willing to help others, it primarily comes from a need to feel good themselves. *(I'm also not saying you should be selfish about some things! By all means, be selfish, jealous even, with your time and energy, and put them into the life you want to live.)*

Don't expect heroes to swoop in and get you out of whatever mess you've gotten yourself into. However, you don't need them to; you can do it yourself!

Whatever problems you have—money, health, relationships, lack of confidence—study and learn how to fix them. If you're bad with money, you are one good book and new actions away from being great at it. If you're bad at playing piano, you're several YouTube videos away from learning the basics and practices away from getting really good at it. Superman can't make you a good piano player. Wonder Woman can't make you a great figure skater.

Batman can't help you increase revenues in your business.

But you can.

Three years ago, I didn't have a shot in hell at getting Pete Vargas, the man who has trained the top speakers in the world, to write the foreword for me. How could he? He didn't know me! I changed that when I took it upon myself to enroll in his online course, then flew to his boot camp in Florida, and then enrolled in more of his activities—all the while playing all-out. I didn't just want to be a fan, though; I wanted to be his friend.

I would keep tabs on his work and send him congratulations when deserved or well wishes when appropriate. While, as of this writing, I can't honestly say I'm at the level where I'm his peer, I can honestly say that we have more than a transactional relationship, proven by his name on this book. Case in point, I didn't wish for him to "save me." I took it upon myself to "save me." My consistent actions caused him to notice me, and I proudly display his endorsement in this book.

No one can hand you courage, skills, abilities, or experience. You have to be intentional about developing those things. The future is coming, and it's up to you which version of you will face it. You can be intentional and *have* it how you want it, or you can be hopeful and *hope* you have it how you want it. I believe God wants you happy, healthy, in great relationships, and fulfilled. I believe the universe will put you in situations to develop the skills you need, since no one will hand them to you. Again, this is a recurring theme in this book for a reason; it's up to you to live the life you want, no one else.

Be the hero in your own movie. Be the star in your own show. Don't rely on superheroes or for someone to save you. You have it in you to save the most important person in the world: yourself.

PLAN A OR PLAN B?

There is a prevailing thought in many circles that I'd like to prescribe to because the warrior in me wants to believe it. That thought is that there must only be a Plan A. If you go into something with a goal in mind, and only that, you'll get it. It's a Burn The Boat mentality derived from the story of the Spanish conquest of the Aztec Empire.

In 1519, Hernan Cortes led a large expedition to Mexico. The goal was to capture a magnificent treasure said to be there. The story goes that upon arrival, Cortes destroyed his ships; he burned his own boats. The message to his men was clear: we will either win or die here. There was no turning back. Two years later, in 1521, Cortes and his men conquered the Aztec Empire.

There are other stories of Burn the Boats; some trace it to Genghis Kahn and others to the time of the ancient Greeks, but regardless of who gets the credit for it, "Burn the boats" has been the battle cry to go all-in—win or die. Even the great Tony Robbins says, "If you want to take the island, you need to burn the boats!"

"Burn the boats" is not just a motivational saying; it's also a helpful concept when making pivots in a business. For example, many years ago, Kodak had to burn its boats when it transitioned from selling film products to offering digital services. Also, when the CEO of Kimberly-Clark made a strategic decision to sell his company's paper mills and invest the money in brands like Kleenex and Huggies, he was ridiculed by the media. However, Darwin E Smith's burn-the-boats move paid off when Kimberly-Clark outperformed Proctor & Gamble and gained complete control of Scott Paper.

I get the burn-the-boats theory. I do. The problem is, at times, Plan A doesn't always work out. Cortes didn't add a thousand men or invent more effective weapons by burning his ships. If you study the Spanish conquest of the Aztec Empire, you'd know that many other factors aided in his victory, such as the coalition of Spanish invaders (not just him and his men) and some of the Aztecs' indigenous enemies and rivals that helped the Spaniards win that war.

John Maxwell says that the difference between a leader and a manager is that a manager will stick to Plan A, regardless of what's going on. On the other hand, a leader will walk behind and in front of the people, leading and altering the plan whenever necessary. Mike Tyson said it best: "Everyone has a plan until they get punched in the face!"

Life will throw you curveballs. If you continue to strike out, you must change your stance or swing higher or lower. You have to know when it's time to try something new. A fly that bumps its head against a window, thinking it will escape if it just doesn't quit and tries harder, will die there.

Knowledge is power, but only when it's used. As you attempt to replace your old habits with newer, better ones, take the time to assess if your new habits are ones you enjoy. The goal of this book is not to change the life you have for the one you want but hate! If Plan A is about getting up earlier and going to the gym, but it's difficult for you to get up, and instead of going to the gym four times a week, you're now going once—change Plan A! Create a Plan B that will have you going to gym right after work or an hour after dinner.

You have to be smart enough to replace your bad habits with new ones that you enjoy or can endure long enough until they become a habit. Stick to Plan A and don't give up on it unless you realize it's just not working. Then, with the new information you've learned about yourself, create a Plan B and stick to that one. Remember, Life will not get you what you want but what you deserve. Basically burn-the-boats means don't ever give up on your goals and alter the plans as needed as you get new information.

ACTION STEPS:

Write down your plan.

Take the vision you have created and bring it all the way back to the steps you need to take right now. Write down the first step, then take action on it right now. Then the second step, and third, and so on.

11
CONSCIOUS VS. SUBCONSCIOUS

To worry is to pray for what you do NOT want.

— *SHARON LECHTER*

STANDARDS

What are your standards? A standard, in some respects, means something so excellent, it cannot be overcome. It means establishing a level of excellence in whatever activity or job you do. A standard is something not easily achieved but something that you wouldn't settle for less than.

I ask again, what are your standards? Have you consciously thought about that? Have you ever written down the things you will and will not negotiate—negotiables and non-negotiables? If not, you either don't have any standards or your standards change often, which is why you're not content with, or proud of, many areas of life.

Your standards, or lack thereof, infiltrate your belief system and mold who and what you are. If you don't have standards, you're whimsical. You may think that you're a go-with-the-flow type of person, but the reality is you don't know what the hell you want, so you let other people or situations decide what you do more than *you* do.

Having talent or being skillful has no bearing on what your standard is. You may be moderately or wildly successful but still not have a standard that governs you. This is why you're constantly searching for new things, shiny toys, and celebrity friends to prove that you have a successful life when, in reality, you're not content. You may have money but not wealth. You may drive a fancy car with a full tank, but your inside is a junker, and your feelings are empty. You may have a large, lavish home, but your heart is lonely.

BE CONSCIOUS

Your standard has turned into your habits, which have materialized into your present-day life, your present-day self. If you believe you should have done more in life than you have, there is still time. First, you need to make a conscious effort to visualize the person you want to be.

Write down:

What you want to be.
Where you want to live.
What friends you want to have.
How much money you make.
How your body looks—health-wise.

Then, go further. Write out a day in your life five years from now. What bed do you wake up in? What do you do first thing —go to a gym, take a walk, reply to emails, meditate? Who's the first person you talk to? Are you greeted with a kiss? What's the conversation about before you head to work? Who are you meeting with that day? How excited are you for that meeting?

Be conscious of the person you want to be. It's impossible to become the person you wish to be without knowing who you want to be. That takes conscious, intentional, introspective thought. Once you know who you want to be, create an emotional connection with that person. What would that person do in certain situations? How would that person talk? How would that person spend any free time? Be mindful of stopping what you would typically do, and be intentional about doing what the person you want to be would do.

Being conscious means being in control. It means that as an intelligent, thinking being, you purposefully do something or don't do it; you deliberately say something or don't say anything.

The most significant act of having free will is being conscious of making a decision.

Being conscious is having power, but don't be fooled; your true power comes from the subconscious.

THE SUBCONSCIOUS

Various Internet sources have deduced that we make approximately 35,000 decisions a day. That's a lot! Thankfully for our poor brains, a far majority of those decisions are made at the subconscious level.

While the brain, the conscious part of you, is tasked with making quite a few decisions—whether to call your mother or if you call her, how much truth to tell her, if you wear the blue tie or the red one, to keep Netflix streaming into the fifth episode of your new favorite show, to color your hair, to take the pizza out of the oven before the house smells like smoke, to follow someone in a crowded parking lot or to keep circling—it's the subconscious part of you that truly dictates your life.

The conscious person you are has chosen to do certain things repeatedly, so much so that it has created a habit. Now, that habit, along with all your other habits, has left the valley of the conscious mind and landed on the subconscious mind. The decisions made at this level go mostly undetected by the conscious mind.

Your subconscious controls the automatic tendencies you have. Some people think they inherit their quick tempers of their quick-tempered fathers through their DNA. Not true. Your conscious mind saw that behavior exemplified repeatedly, and you then agreed with being that way and began to exhibit the same patterns. You did it consistently, and today—well, you're a hot-head, like your father, but not because he was your father; it's because you chose to be, absolving you from any part of it and blaming it on your father.

The relationship between the conscious mind and the subconscious is incredibly complex, yet easy to understand. The conscious mind elects to do things repeatedly until the subconscious takes them off the hands of the conscious mind and allows the conscious mind to think about other things, while the subconscious mind dictates the actions taken.

We have all trained our subconscious minds on what to look out for. For example, if you're a musician and walk into my kitchen, you'll probably not notice much of what's in my kitchen, and instead gravitate to one of the guitars hanging on the wall of a nearby room. However, if you were a refrigerator repairman, you wouldn't notice the hanging guitars, but instead, the irregular humming of my refrigerator. If you were an interior decorator, you wouldn't notice the guitar or the fridge humming because you'd wonder why the hell I chose such a color scheme.

The things you pick out are things you have told your subconscious are important. If you are in tune with how you spend your money, it's because you've told your subconscious, through repeated action, that financial literacy is essential.

What things do you notice?
What things do people tell you that you never notice?
What things would you like to notice?

CONSISTENCY AND BELIEF

The problem many people have is that they carry a stigma, a belief, a history into something which complicates it. If you want to quit drinking because your wife tells you that you should, but the two of you fight half the time, you put the cause of your drinking on her. The emotional connection to sobriety is not strong enough to create new habits. If you were to change the belief and quit drinking because you're sick and tired of waking up with a hangover and ashamed of how you've acted while intoxicated, you'd have the foundational fuel to get you through the long journey to sobriety.

Here's a news flash: you can make things matter more than they do or less than they do. The best way to change is to take negative emotions attached to something and turn them into positive emotions. The step-by-step process of creating a new habit or replacing an old one shouldn't rely on emotions alone. It's all about consistency and belief.

Consistency is greater than intensity. Intensity wanes, and motivation fades over time.

People governed by emotions face the harsh law of diminishing returns. Sure, you'll start like a bat out of hell, but sooner or later, you won't have the same level of urgency until, inevitably, the new action you wanted to do lies in the wasteland of the many other things you were excited to do.

Do you really want to change for the better? Be consistent. That's it! Just do it, and then do it again, and then again, and again, and then again. Make your new standard: "I am a person who keeps promises to myself." Do it on Monday. Do it on Wednesday. Do it on Friday. Do it every morning. Do it five times a week. Just be consistent.

The path to greatness starts with consistency. The greatest athletes didn't focus on every sport, just the ones they became great at. Michael Jordan was one of the most gifted athletes of my generation. Yet, his greatness didn't follow him when he left basketball for baseball. He got so good at basketball that, in one particular game, he closed his eyes in front of thirty thousand people in a stadium and millions of others watching on TV and made a free throw. This tells me that he must have taken hundreds of thousands of free throws. Swimming legend Michael Phelps didn't leave swimming and win tournaments in tennis. Greatness, my friend, begins with vision and belief, but is reached through consistency.

You must believe you are capable and deserving of the life you want. Your Belief System, which this book is about, has dictated your life to where it is now and will dictate the life you'll live in the future. It's not your Think System; it's your Belief System. Doubt will come. Fear will attack. Anxiety, incredulity, and loathing hide around the corner—only belief beats them.

When a person is one hundred percent certain that they can do a thing, that thing almost always gets done. When a person is one hundred percent certain that they can't do something, that thing never gets done. If you don't believe you deserve a great life, you won't have one. If you don't believe you can run a 5K, you'll never go out and start walking, and then run a little every day, and then run 2 miles, and then 3, and then the 5K.

Stop wishing and start believing. Stop wishing you could have a life like your successful brother, a marriage like your spoiled cousin, a physique like your stud best friend—believe you can, make a decision to take small consistent actions, repeat "I am" or "I have" statements, and you will create the life you desire! Once you believe you can do a thing, you will find the way to start doing the things that will get you there.

ACTION STEPS:

Write down what you are going to say to your subconscious mind, with emotion and certainty. Use statements that start with I am or I have.

For Example; I am someone who keeps promises to myself. I have the discipline to repeat successful actions. Etc…

Write down what your new beliefs are and repeat it 3 times per day.

12

R.I.P

If you think the price of discipline is high, wait until you get the bill of regret.

— JIM ROHN

HOMICIDE

A few years ago when I made the conscious decision to be intentional about who I wanted to become it meant that I had to "kill" my former self. I had to morph in to a new person all together. Changing myself from the caterpillar to a butterfly. In a sense you have to kill the old beliefs, thought processes, and habits to make room for the new ones. No one can stay the same and change. Their internal reality has to change first and then the external reality will change.

You will have to do the same. You are going to "kill" your current fears and limitations so that you can fly.

You may not know it, but the current you is at war with the better version of you that you can be.

It's time to stop being so damn friendly with someone who will do everything in their power to keep you from evolving.

Retrospection. Introspection. Projection.

RETROSPECTION

Reanalyze the events of your past and the definitions you've given them.

There are things in your life that you've made conclusions about and those conclusions have become your belief system. It is who you are today. You may have made decisions when you were eleven years old that direct your emotions and actions against a particular thing. You may be twenty, thirty-five, or sixty, but when that specific thing comes up, you still act like an eleven-year-old.

It's time to act your age! Meaning: look back at the events of your past and realize that the events that occurred are emotion-less; they are simply events that happened, and it was you who put the emotions into them. Now, as an adult, I ask you to go back to those memories from a different perspective, being that you now have much more life experience, and evaluate if those feelings are still valid. If they aren't, flip the switch in your brain to react to them differently if something similar happens.

We primarily view our lives as heroes or victims. When we do something good and tell the story, we are heroes. We love to hear the compliments and get the pats on the back. When things don't go our way, though, if we say them out loud or just think about them, we find a way to blame someone else, thus becoming the victim.

I challenge you to challenge every time of your life when you have convinced yourself that you were the victim, that you had nothing to do with some of the bad things that may have happened to you. I'm not saying that it's always going to be true, but I would wager that you would lose the victim memory of some things, which would make you stronger today. Put a different emotion in your past and start feeling better in your present.

For example, I love my dad but thought he was overly hard on me. Maybe I'm not the only one who ever thought that. After I did something, he would often respond with, "It's okay, but you know you could've done better." For just about everything I did, I would hear, "You can do better." I would sulk in my room as a victim and, for many years, grew up believing that I was not valuable, I never did things good enough, and that, as a result, my time wasn't all too valuable. In short, he made me feel I wasn't worth much. In retrospect, when I look back at those times, I'm grateful for them. They made me strong. They taught me to strive harder and to push through. Heck, I became a doctor! Now that I have my own experiences as a father and try to motivate my children, I realize that he was trying to be the best dad he could be. I don't know; my kids might feel that way toward me at times, but I never tell them something that does not come from a place of advice from a loving father.

INTROSPECTION

Look internally and decide if your current beliefs are valid or not.

Beliefs come from decisions you've made with information you had at the time. New beliefs are new decisions because you've believed in new information. I'll tell you right now, the first step to improvement is understanding who you are at this very moment and what you believe. What are your strengths? Some people also ask what are your weaknesses, except that I don't like to call them weaknesses. I call them opportunities to grow and improve.

What areas do you need support in to understand yourself better? What triggers have gone vigilante on you and taken over your emotions without you being able to stop it?

You decide to be a slave to your feelings or to master them.

When you're too emotional, you lose control; people's actions control you, words from others control you, and situations that don't even deal with you control you. When you don't have control you are a slave to your surroundings.

Find out who you are. I recommend you take an assessment test. My favorite is the DISC Assessment. Trust me; it's worth the time and small monetary investment to objectively understand yourself without your bias and emotions muddying up the waters. What are your standards? What are your non-negotiables, or do you not have any?

Find out how you react under stress and your good and bad tendencies so you can be aware of them and make better decisions. Better decisions, better life.

PROJECTION

Envision your future and feel what that person feels

Go back to Step #1 of the five steps to living a great life and create the imaginary, emotional person you want to be in a future time. How does that person talk? How would that person react to bad news? Who does that person confide in? Who does that person go to for counsel? What time does that person wake up? What is their morning routine? What are the emotions they experience most of the time? How good does it feel to be trustworthy? How good does it feel not to need financial assistance from anyone? How do you feel getting out of that car?

Reprogram the Reticular Activating System in your brain and attract the things you need in order to make that imaginary person the one to look back at you in the mirror. Create the imaginary, emotional person of your future, and your current person will figure out where to go and how to find what it needs to be that person. You must become that person inside before you manifest that person to the world.

Some people think if they have enough money, they'll be rich. While some would agree, I tell you this: they would not stay rich for long. You need to think like the rich to be and remain rich. Giving a lot of money to people with a poverty mentality will not change their lives, but changing from a poverty mentality to one of abundance certainly will. Have you ever known someone you thought would "make it" or be famous one day? It's because that person is already acting like it, but his or her future self hasn't caught up in the present time with his or her destined reality.

The Five Steps

1. Create the vision of the person you want to become. Don't worry about the HOW; just tap into your innermost self and figure out the WHO.
2. Identify the habits that bring you to that person. Defend those habits, fight for them, and strengthen them. Make them non-negotiable.

3. Identify the habits that take you away from becoming that person. You can't win a war if you don't know who you are fighting.

4. Create alternate habits from those that take you away from becoming that person. Replace old beliefs that produced terrible habits with new beliefs founded with new information, and build new, better habits.

5. Take Action. Writing them down is a good start, but consistently challenging yourself for just thirty days will embed those new, better habits.

The future you is calling out to the present you, begging you to be strong. If he or she could talk to you, you'd hear that the juice is worth the squeeze. The prize is definitely worth the effort.

One more writing assignment. I'd like you to imagine yourself twelve months from now and envision how your life would be if you took action on things you've learned in this book. Imagine yourself three years from now, five years from now. Write down: How does your life look? What are you driving? What fears have you eliminated? What habits have you erased, and which habits have you created? Visualize it, and write it down. Write down the best life you have the potential to live if you have the courage to eliminate the habits that keep you from your dream life. Create and consistently act on the new habits that bring you closer to your goals.

Read it over and over again. Continue to visualize an amazing future, because the more you advance, the more your goals will change. Never delete goals you've written and obtained; list them as achieved. This will give you more strength, more fuel for the journey ahead. You really are the master of your destiny, but you have to stop hitting the snooze button of your life and get up.

I hope this book spoke to you in ways you could not have imagined. However, I can't help change your life with a book or a speech. I can only plant a seed. What you do with it, if and when you water it, must be a conscious effort on your part. If you'd like to continue working with me to develop the person you want to be, you can find me at www.fixyourbs.com.

Join me for my weekly coaching calls, and find out when my following mastermind events will be. Plug in. Devote to yourself and give the world an amazing gift—the best you.

ACTION STEPS:

Put the whole book together and write down an action intention statement of who you intend to become and what you are committed to doing starting now.

Share this intention statement with me on social media @fixyourbs @drgregpursley

FIX YOUR B.S.

ABOUT THE AUTHOR

Dr. Greg Pursley – aka Dr. G. – is a highly successful entrepreneur and businessman who helps others achieve their dream lives through practical exercises stemming from his personal experiences and mentoring.

As a young man, he lived on a farm, raced motocross, and worked with his dad, an electrician, where he learned the value of hard work and discipline.

He attended Chiropractic College and received a doctorate at 23 years old. He married his wife, Sheree, and they had their first child, a daughter named Evee-Kay.

Shortly thereafter, he moved two hours away and opened his practice.

Two years later, their son Izaac was born. Izaac was born with dwarfism, a random and rare genetic change in the third trimester of pregnancy. This created a significant shift in his family's life. Izaac suffered many medical complications and spent six months of his first year in the hospital. He would require a tracheotomy and ventilator to help him breathe for the next eight years. Dr. Pursley focused on keeping the family together and keeping Izaac alive.

When Izaac's condition stabilized, Dr. G. found himself in a difficult situation. Everything was in disarray; his finances, relationships, health, career, and faith were all suffering. He felt as if he was drowning, as if he had lost. It was at this moment that he went on a search to find his dream life.

Dr. G.'s first book, Fix Your B.S., teaches the processes he used to create the life he wanted – the type of life that excited him. Now a best-selling author, Dr. G. is one of the most highly sought-after speakers in the world. His goal is to continue to help change millions of lives for the better.

To follow or contact Dr. G to speak at your event, go to www.-fixyourbs.com.

ACKNOWLEDGMENTS

Thank you to my wife and children for having faith in me even when I doubted myself and to the countless mentors who were there to guide me, teach me, and help me see my true potential.

RECOMMENDED READING

I highly recommend these books, they have changed my life!

- Think and Grow Rich: Napoleon Hill
- Beyond Positive Thinking: Dr. Robert Anthony
- The Power of Positive Thinking: Normal Vincent Peale
- The Power of One More Ed: Mylett
- Becoming a Person of Influence: John Maxwell
- Outwitting the Devil: Napoleon Hill and Sharon Lechter
- Awaken The Giant Within: Tony Robbins
- The Untethered Soul: Michael Alan Singer
- You Were Born Rich: Bob Proctor
- The 10X Rule: Grant Cordone
- You Are a Badass at Making Money: Jen Sincero
- As a Man Thinketh: James Allen
- 7 Habits of Highly Effective People: Stephen R Covey
- The Richest Man in Babylon: George Samuel Clason
- Atomic Habits: James Clear
- Don't Believe Everything You Think: Joseph Nguyen
- The Speed of Trust: William R Covey

RECOMMENDED READING

- What Got You Here Won't Get You There: Marshal Goldsmith
- The 5 Love Languages: Gary Chapman
- How to Win Friends and Influence People: Dale Carnegie
- Everything is Figureoutable: Marie Forleo
- Life Force: Tony Robbins